FLYFISHING
IN IRELAND

PETER O'REILLY

FLYFISHING
IN IRELAND

PETER O'REILLY

Sponsored by the
CENTRAL FISHERIES BOARD
IRELAND

MERLIN UNWIN BOOKS

First published in Great Britain by Merlin Unwin Books, 2000

ISBN 1 873674 35 X

Text © Peter O'Reilly
Illustrations © Charles Jardine

Published by
Merlin Unwin Books
Palmers House
7 Corve Street, Ludlow
Shropshire SY8 1DB
U.K.

British Library Cataloguing-in-Publication Data:
A catalogue record for this book is available from the British Library.

Designed by H D Communications, Ludlow
Printed in Spain by Zure S.A.

CONTENTS

To Rose

for her unfailing support

A reassuring message for all who go fishing – the door of a fishing hut on the River Slaney in County Wexford

FOREWORD
JOHN O'CONNOR

After joining the Central Fisheries Board, I learned that Peter O'Reilly had produced a pamphlet on casting. On reading it, I was immediately struck by the potential for a more detailed treatment of flyfishing in the Irish context. I discussed this with Peter. He concurred and readily agreed to undertake this challenging project.

A publisher was required to bring it to fruition. Peter approached Merlin Unwin who published his three previous highly successful books – *Rivers of Ireland, Loughs of Ireland* and *Flies of Ireland*. Merlin agreed and the result of this collaborative endeavour is a unique and valuable contribution to flyfishing in Ireland.

The book is primarily intended for those wishing to improve their knowledge of flyfishing in Ireland as well as beginners wishing to improve their knowledge and techniques. It is instructive, informative and practical and draws on the author's professional expertise and encyclopaedic knowledge of the sport. Methods and techniques of flyfishing are outlined in great detail as well as the kind of flies and tackle required for the best results. The text is very readable, with interesting anecdotes and interspersed with helpful illustrations and skilful artwork.

Two of my board's principal objectives are to make angling attractive and accessible to our young people, and to promote it abroad. I believe this book will make a major contribution in this regard. We have some of the best wild brown trout, salmon and sea trout fishing in the world and this book will contribute greatly to enhancing people's enjoyment of this unique, natural resource. I congratulate Peter on this fine work and have no doubt that it will achieve great success.

John O'Connor
Chief Executive
Central Fisheries Board
Dublin 9

ACKNOWLEDGEMENTS

There is always something new to be learned about fly fishing. Indeed, at a time when there is so much emphasis on 'life long learning', the riverbank could be considered to be one of the first such academies. Practically every time we go fishing we observe something different. It is my hope that this book will serve the dual purpose of both providing answers to some of the questions I get asked by Irish anglers, as well as informing anglers from overseas of the conditions they are likely to meet and the methods and tactics required.

There is so much to be learned, I sometimes feel that I haven't passed that far beyond the beginners' stage. The list of helpful anglers who have advised me along the way is a long one with many special memories. I would like to thank them all including my colleagues in the former Inland Fisheries Trust and the Central and Regional Fisheries Boards. Several sadly, are no longer with us. Many were especially helpful and some must be singled out for special mention. Apart from my mother, Cissie and father, Patrick, and Hughie Sheridan, who got me started, there was Sean Kettle, Rev. Michael Fox, Eddie Gorman, Mick Finnigan, Peter Gaffney, Sean and Mary Young, Ronnie Lyttle, Lal and Mary Faherty, John O'Connor, Michael Conneelly, Peter Mantle, Kieran Thomson, Michael Kelly, James Rooney, Robert Gillespie, Tommy McCutcheon and Mike Weaver.

I wish to take this opportunity to acknowledge the encouragement I received from Mr John O'Connor, C.E.O., Central Fisheries Board and my thanks to the Board for its support.

Merlin Unwin is the kindest, most patient, courteous and tolerant of publishers. My gratitude is due to him and his team, including Charles Jardine and Peter Owen for the illustrations and Tony Deacon who kindly read the typescript.

I am exceedingly grateful to Ms Bridie Fleming and my son Patrick who typed the copy, for the care and trouble that they took.

To all who have been generous with their time and advice, I offer my sincere thanks.

Peter O'Reilly

PHOTO ACKNOWLEDGEMENTS

Many people have kindly allowed me to reproduce their photos in this book and I wish to thank them all warmly. In particular: Valentine Atkinson (pages 14, 54, 62, 66, 74, 150, 155), Jon Beer (pages 30, 31), Bord Failte (page 58), Michael Browne (page 122), Rod Calbrade (pages 27, 38, 130, 154), Terry Griffiths (pages 35, 79, 119, 147), Stuart McTeare (pages 72, 82, 90, 91, 92, 94, 99, 102, 158), Jim Repine (pages 22), Tilman Schuppius (pages 37, 162), Paul Sheehan (pages 6, 10, 71, 101, 123, 127, 131, 134, 135, 161), Mike Weaver (pages 42, 50), John Wilshaw (pages 13, 15, 70, 86, 95, 99, 106, 111, 138, 139, 159).

INTRODUCTION

PETER O'REILLY

In over fifty years' fishing, I have never met a skilful, all round angler who would not prefer to fish with a fly when it is practical. Originally, people fished the fly only for salmon and trout. Nowadays, people are flyfishing for pike, coarse fish and many species of sea fish.

What is it that makes flyfishing so interesting? Firstly, catching a fish on a fly is very much the angler's own responsibility. You see a fish or know where it lies, choose the fly, tie it on, make the cast, control the line and the fly. Then you hook, play and land the fish all by yourself. Secondly, there is the joy you get out of casting. Controlling a flyline in the air and presenting a fly well is pure joy. Using a bait rod does not compare. Some get their enjoyment out of golf or tennis or clay-pigeon shooting. Spin fishing can certainly be fun and, on its day, effective. But for me, fly casting and flyfishing are pure enjoyment.

YOU CAN DO IT!

Unfortunately, there is a belief, held by many, that unless you are blessed with exceptional gifts of co-ordination, you will never learn to cast a fly well. Nothing could be further from the truth. In fact, any normally co-ordinated person can learn to cast a fly rod after a few lessons from a competent teacher and a bit of practice. It is best to take casting lessons from a qualified instructor. We all have enough faults without adding to them by learning those of a bad teacher!

There is always something new to learn in flyfishing. This is one of the fascinations of the sport. Some things we discover for ourselves, but mostly we learn through sharing experiences with fellow anglers. It was such an incident that prompted me to begin tying my own flies.

It was eight o'clock in the morning and I had just arrived back at the jetty, almost fishless despite fishing a good early morning rise of trout. Further down the shore, another boat slid up on the gravel and two anglers climbed ashore. We exchanged pleasantries in the warm morning sunshine. Each of them had caught several trout while I had struggled to catch just one, a fraction over the size limit. We had both fished in the same area of the lough and covered the same rising trout. They were successful and I was not. Obviously, they were doing something different. But I was too proud to ask. Then, as I finished packing the gear away in the car boot, one of them walked over, placed a match box on the bonnet of the car and said, 'The fly we caught all the fish on is in that match box'. I thanked her. She had made my day and I could only marvel at how generous some people can be. I took the fly home, tied up an imitation and returned to the lough that same evening for the evening rise. Now I caught five trout and came

OVERLEAF
Delphi Lodge, one of Ireland's foremost fishing establishments, seen across the crystal clear waters of Fin Lough.

away feeling chuffed, satisfied, fulfilled and all because of a fellow angler's generosity and willingness to share their experience.

Incidentally, the fly in question was a Kingsmill, not the easiest of flies to tie and not one that I would recommend for your first attempt at tying.

It is now more than fifty years since I first watched trout and salmon and minnows and gudgeon in the clear water of the river Annalee and listened to the pulsing sound of the water wheel of my father's corn mill. When spring came, I watched fishermen, from a distance, catch trout with their bright yellow cane rods. I can still see in the mind's eye the writhing and jumping golden bellied half-pounders as they were unceremoniously hauled up the gravel bank. I too wanted to be a fisherman. Soon I was off to the hazel grove to cut myself a fishing rod.

Over a long fishing life, I have picked up a lot of excellent advice. Like most human activity, a huge store of knowledge and information on angling has been built up. What other human activity has produced such wonderful literature? The information already exists. It is a matter of being able to find it. There is no need to invent the wheel all over again. Very few of us make original discoveries. It has been my experience that there is very little new in fishing. Recently I learned that the supposedly new English wonder fly of the 1960s – the Black & Peacock Spider – already existed under a different name at the end of the last century in Ireland.

BEWARE OF THE EXPERT

It is important to keep an open mind in fishing. We have to learn to distinguish between the mindlessly repeated dogma of those who cannot be bothered to think intelligently about their fishing and the store of useful traditional knowledge that we neglect at our peril. We must always be prepared to continue to build on our experience. When asked for advice on the choice of a fly for a given situation, I am loath to suggest any specific one, let alone declare that it never fails. Rather, I prefer to suggest a selection and then say that if all else fails, I always fall back on one or two favourite patterns.

We must beware of angling experts. A good friend once advised that there is no such thing as an angling expert – only self-proclaimed ones. That may be so, but nonetheless, my dictionary defines an expert as 'someone having a special skill or knowledge'. Now, there's a thought. The problem in assessing a fishing expert is that fishing is as much an art as a science and as such, it defies precise evaluation. Which takes me back to the store of knowledge and information that has been built up over the years. Really, what we have are general rules that have been known to work in most situations. One expert may claim that a particular fly never fails. That may be so, fished the way he fishes it in his river or lough. But it may not succeed for anyone else. Indeed, it may be a total failure because fishing conditions are so variable. This holds true for any specific fly or technique. In science, conclusions are reached by conducting and repeating experiments under identical conditions, but in fishing this is

A brace of perfect Irish lough trout, full-bellied and with large dark spots. The angling heritage we must be sure to pass on to the next generation.

impossible because conditions are so variable. They may appear identical to the last visit we made to the lough or river, but in scientific terms they are not. There are always minute variations which may, or may not, affect the behaviour of the fish. The cloud formation may be denser or lighter; the water or air temperature may be a degree up or down; the wind a little stronger or lighter or coming at a slightly different angle; the oxygen content of the water may be different: the permutations are endless and for all practical purposes, it can be assumed that they are never exactly the same. This being so, proof of the effectiveness of any particular fly or technique is impossible.

The most we can hope for and the best we can do is to apply general rules that experience has taught us will work in average situations. The consolation here is that the beginner can succeed where the old hand fails and everyone can be an expert on his day. However, my feeling is that experience and constant practice make for more consistent success.

Evening success on Sheelin. After a long day in the boat, this 4-pounder came to the spent gnat just as the light was failing.

A GIFT TO TREASURE

As we enter the third millennium, our thoughts turn to the environment. Fish and the water they swim in are very much a part of our environment. The wild trout and salmon stocks in our rivers and loughs are a priceless asset. Ireland is fortunate to still have the luxury of relatively good stocks of salmon and trout and Irish anglers are blessed in being able to fish for them in their natural surroundings. Indeed, were it not for the strenuous efforts of anglers and the Fishery Boards over the last twenty five years in the fight against water pollution and stream degradation, stocks would not be so plentiful. In a world where more and more people want to fish, we have to be careful not to harm or damage our wild fish population. Where trout and salmon are concerned, we should realise that their numbers are limited and that only a small percentage of the fry population ever survive to maturity. As fishing tackle becomes ever more sophisticated and anglers more efficient and effective, we are in danger of reducing stocks to such an extent that fisheries, especially our trout rivers, may cease to be worth fishing. Indeed, the process is already happening and I have experience of taking young anglers out to teach them to fish only to find the river denuded of trout by thoughtless, greedy early season fishers.

If we are all to continue to enjoy our sport in the future, it will be necessary for everyone to adopt conservation measures that the older generation of anglers, used to carrying home bags of fish, may at first find difficult to accept. But there is no real alternative because if too many anglers kill too many fish, the result will be poorer sport all round.

The classic 'sonaghan' markings: black fins and tail, grey underbelly and black spots. They will often feed avidly at the surface.

After spending much time pondering this new problem facing the game fisher, I was pleased to come across an American angling organisation called 'Trout Unlimited'. Their philosophy seems to me to be eminently wise and I commend it to you:

> 'We believe that trout and salmon fishing isn't just fishing for trout and salmon. It is fishing for sport rather than for food, where the true enjoyment of the sport lies in the challenge, the lure, and the battle of wits, not necessarily the full creel. It is the feeling of satisfaction that comes from limiting your kill instead of killing your limit. It is communing with nature, where the chief reward is a refreshed body and a contented soul, where a license is a permit to use, not abuse; to enjoy, not destroy our coldwater fishery. It is subscribing to the proposition that what's good for trout and salmon is good for fishermen and that managing trout and salmon for themselves rather than for the fishermen is fundamental to the solution of our trout and salmon problems. It is appreciating our fishery resource, respecting fellow anglers and giving serious thought to tomorrow'.

I thoroughly commend the above sentiments to all who read the following pages and I hope that you too will practice Trout Unlimited's philosophy more widely. We are fortunate that in Ireland we have thousands of streams and hundreds of rivers and loughs capable of producing and sustaining stocks of wild trout and salmon that are the envy of anglers the world over. They are a precious inheritance for us to enjoy but we also have the responsibility to hand them on undiminished to the next generation. Anything less is too terrible to contemplate. The ultimate indignity would be to condemn the next generation to fish for stocked fish in a fishery that should be capable of producing, nurturing and sustaining wild fish. It would be a real tragedy. By practising 'catch and release' we are investing in its future. I wonder if that was what that great lover of the animals and the birds – and no doubt the fish – Francis of Assisi had in mind when he counselled that 'It is better to give than to receive'. Go on, give your next fish a second chance. 'A salmon or trout is too valuable to be only caught once', said the great American angler, Lee Wulff.

THE LUCKY FLYFISHER

While my fishing nowadays is almost exclusively confined to flyfishing – and I get great satisfaction from teaching others to flyfish – it was not always so. It all began with that hazel rod, mentioned earlier, freshly cut in the wood. Next there was the modified tank aerial and a fixed spool reel attached but there was always the lure of the trout on a fly and the memory of those men with the maroon-whipped Hardy cane rods which I admired while they had their lunch of ham sandwiches washed down by tea from a thermos flask.

My opportunity to flyfish came when I received a present of a fly rod from a dear old friend, my parish priest. A short time later another friend took me fishing with the admonition that 'the man who fishes for trout with a worm is lower than the worm he fishes with'.

I was about to learn to flyfish, and I did. It has brought me a lot of satisfaction, taken me to many stunningly beautiful locations and made me a lot of friends.

When you catch a good trout or finally beach a heavy salmon, is it the reward of skill or luck? It may be a little of both but it might be more illuminating to approach the question from another viewpoint. To attribute success in flyfishing to luck alone is as unsatisfactory as it is to try to make it into an exact science whereby you do 'this' and 'that' and the result is always a fish. Better by far to approach the question from the position of the traditional angling skills. They are:

(1) Observation
(2) Rivercraft
(3) Fly selection
(4) Fly casting

It is by honing and perfecting these four skills that the fly angler achieves success. It is with the practice of these skills that the flyfisher is mainly concerned. From them, he or she will derive the greatest of pleasure and the hooking and landing of a fish is the ultimate bonus.

For reasons of clarity I have, throughout this book, expressed the common names of natural insects in small letters (eg. duck fly) but the corresponding artificial starting with a capital letter (eg. Duck fly). If at times I have referred to the angler as 'he' it is merely for the sake of simplicity and not, I can assure female readers, through an ingrained male chauvinism. Many of the finest anglers in Ireland are women.

I am quite aware of the difficulties involved in trying to instruct in flyfishing from a book. Some will say 'You can't learn to fish from a book' and they may well be right. 'Hands on' experience is certainly important, but there is much you can learn about flyfishing from the written word. It is good to know how and why certain principles work, what to look out for and things to do and practice. A knowledge of these things can make the difference between success and failure. Ireland offers a wide range of challenges to the flyfisher and if you can, for example, see at a glance when to fish the Klinkhämer for river trout, a floating bloodworm on the lough, or a mini-tube for salmon, you will be ahead of the posse. I hope this book goes some way in guiding you towards meeting these challenges and that you will get boundless enjoyment from your flyfishing in Ireland.

Peter O'Reilly
Ballybatter House
Boyne Hill, Navan
Co. Meath
Ireland

June 2000

1

FISHING THE WET FLY FOR RIVER TROUT

lyfishing on rivers falls into two categories: fishing the rise or
fishing the water. In the former, locating the trout is easy. They
give their presence away by rising and leaving tell-tale rings on the
surface. But it is not always so and when there are no signs in
evidence, then we must 'fish the water', using wet flies or nymphs to search
the water in the hope of a take.

For sheer excitement and enjoyment, this is a form of fishing that is
hard to surpass. It is probably also one of the easiest forms of fishing to
master and ideal for the beginner. Basically, in its simplest form, the angler
casts the flies on the water which carries them along and around in its flow.
A trout then sees them, fancies one for a meal, snaps it up and, before the
angler knows, he has hooked a trout. For many anglers, this is their first
experience of flyfishing. It is easy to see how they get 'hooked'. Everything
is quiet and peaceful, the angler wrapped up in his thoughts, probably
admiring how well the last cast landed when, like an electric shock, the rod
in his hand shudders and at the end of the line is a protesting, angry,
leaping trout.

Even for the seasoned river angler, fishing the water with the wet fly
or nymph is full of expectation. Come the first days of March, with the
trees still bare and the bankside vegetation laid low, a rusty brown after the
winter frost, wet flyfishing is the most likely method to produce a trout.
Now a wild brown trout from the river is a beautiful fish and the first one
of the season is particularly so. So also is the novice angler's first trout.

To become a proficient trout angler requires the acquisition of a
certain amount of knowledge about the fish's life cycle and habitat, as well
as acquiring fishing skills. There is a great mass of literature available on
trout, their world and their habits, but it is not necessary to become a scientist in order to fish and enjoy fishing. A little knowledge about the trout and
its environment is all that is needed to begin. From there on, our knowledge can be expanded at the university of the river bank.

Trout live in a complex watery world. The fact that it is watery makes

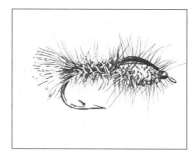  

it both interesting and mysterious. Interesting, because they live in a different medium from us and mysterious because we cannot easily observe them.

Brown trout inhabit both rivers and loughs. These two kinds of water differ greatly from each other. Equally, there are different kinds of rivers and differing types of loughs.

The river trout fisher must first find a river that holds trout. Not all rivers and streams do so. Fortunately, we are blessed in this country with a great number of rivers that do hold trout. Indeed, brown trout are the most widespread species of fish in the country.

Trout, like all living creatures, have certain basic requirements in order to survive. These include clean water, oxygen, moderate temperature, food, places to rest in strong currents, shelter from bright sunshine, security from enemies and predators and clean gravel in which to spawn.

Natural rivers, like the river Annalee and its sister, Upper Erne tributaries where I first cast a wet fly, are wonderfully complex places with great diversity. By comparison, a canal is only a bath tub – plain, regular and predictable. A river which has been subjected to a drainage scheme falls somewhere in between. It is often more suited to the dry fly. A good wet fly river will have a varying width, gradient, depth and type of bottom. It is these topographical features or characteristics that determine whether a river holds trout or not and also the average size and number of trout it contains. When the gradient is steep and the water fast over a bottom of rock, stones and boulders, trout are often the only fish species present. They will also be present in large numbers where the flow is rather less fast and the bottom is stony. As the gradient becomes less steep, the numbers often decrease but the average size increases and few trout will be found in either very shallow water or in deep sluggish water with a muddy bottom – but there are exceptions.

The distribution and numbers of trout in a stretch of river are mainly related to its topographical features like gradient, width and the type of the river bed. The type of river bed is important. It is usually made up of gravel, stones and rock or silt, but trout prefer gravel and stones. A stony bottom usually means that the surface of the water is broken, there are good 'lies' or resting places and plenty of food. These are the areas that the angler is always on the look out for.

Variations of the weighted nymph, from left: Gold-ribbed hare's ear, Pheasant tail nymph and PVC nymph.

OBSERVATION

The nature of the gradient and of the river bottom result in different types of water throughout its length. Anglers have names for them such as white water, falls, riffles, runs, streams, glides, flats and pools. Each has its own particular water speed and bottom type. The different types of water hold different sizes and numbers of trout but this can vary with the time of year, for trout have a habit of moving about according to the season or even the time of day. Few, if any, trout will be found in white water or falls but they will rest in pools and pockets at the bottom of falls. Riffles consist of fast shallow water over a stony bottom and usually only hold small trout except at dusk when bigger trout will often move up to the tail of the riffle to feed. Runs, streams and glides have greater depth, a slower current, a plentiful food supply and generally good living conditions. Now good living conditions or good 'lies' usually mean that the trout are numerous and of a good average size. These are the areas the wet fly angler is looking for. Here the trout are plentiful, always on the look-out for the next meal, and the speed of the flow means that they must make hasty decisions when they spot a passing morsel of food carried down on the stream. Usually, if it looks half

A slight bulge on the surface of the water indicates the presence of a big stone, and trout will lie behind, beside and in front of such obstacles

Direction of current

acceptable, they will grab hold of it before one of the neighbours does so. Glide water, flats and deeper pools are less productive to the wet fly. This may be because trout are not as plentiful or because they have more time to observe the fly. But they should not be discounted altogether. Flyfishing is not an exact science and the unexpected is one of its thrills.

Most beginners learn the facts of wet fly river fishing the hard way. They fish every inch of water and soon learn that trout are not evenly spread and that hours can be wasted fishing fishless water. It is then that the realisation dawns: that being observant and keeping one's eyes open pays dividends. Soon the newcomer is able to recognise not only streams, flats and pools but at a glance will spot other features that may cause a concentration of flow which will funnel the trout's food, or a piece of cover, in the form of weed, rocks or overhanging branches, that will make the lie attractive to the fish. Like the grace notes in a melody, these are the things that make for diversity and that challenge the hunting instincts. And those takes, those attacking bites of the trout, come more frequently along the side of a stream or fast run. A slight bulge on the water as it curls away

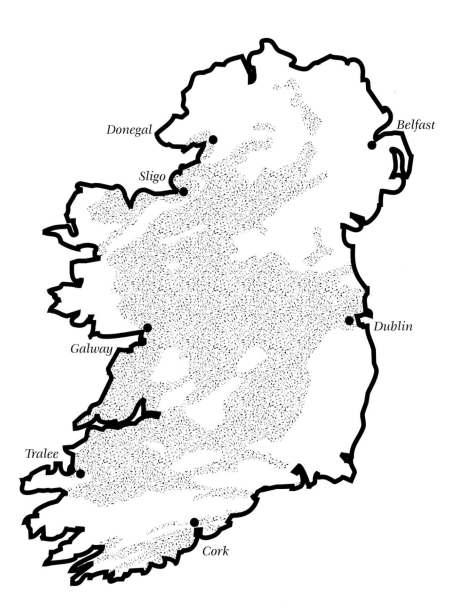

Carboniferous limestone regions of Ireland (shaded in grey) which contain the most productive rivers and loughs in the country.

downstream indicates the presence of a big stone on the bottom and trout like to lie beside, before or behind big stones. A rush of water between two boulders is even better than one on its own and may harbour several trout. The outside of a bend can create a conveyor belt of current carrying food to a number of trout lying head to tail in perfect pecking order. The side of a fallen tree trunk or a trailing bush has much the same effect. It soon becomes quite evident that some places in a river or stream hold more trout than others (see page 145). The best feeding spots amount to only a fraction of the water's total area. The trout are where the food is. They are reluctant to waste energy and become expert at finding positions where the current brings the food near to them. Man unwittingly became their ally too, particularly in the past when he placed stepping stones across rivers, or built small footbridges with pillars of loose stone gathered from the surrounding river bed. The rush of water through the eyes of such structures will have gouged out holes in the gravelly river bottom and a dozen or more good trout may be found lying here. They are eager to take a wet fly in such places when the water height is right. If the river is too high and in flood, the current in the run below the bridge may be too strong and the trout will move up into the glide water above the bridge. If it is too weak – perhaps in high summer – the trout may feel exposed and seek better shelter. A rock ledge across a river is another likely place. An angler may have fished an apparently fishless stretch of water for an hour or more and then he reaches one of these features and, quite unexpectedly, takes come in rapid succession, one after the other. Such are the surprises and unexpected joys of the wet fly river fisher.

Sadly, man has upset the trout's world in a lot of rivers with his drainage works and arterial drainage schemes. In some rivers, the damage done is long term and in a few, practically irreversible. Others have recovered more quickly, aided by the tireless work of dedicated fishery staff, bless them, who build small weirs and shunt boulders about in rivers and streams and generally try to make a home once more for the brown trout.

LOCATING YOUR TROUT RIVER

There is a great diversity of scenery in Ireland due to the geology of the country and, by being observant, it is generally possible to determine those parts of the country likely to contain good trout streams and rivers and those that do not. There is a correlation between the rock structure of the countryside through which a river flows and its ability to produce and maintain a worthwhile stock of trout. Hard, clear alkaline waters produce good numbers of fast-growing quality trout while in soft acid water, the trout are small and stunted.

Hard alkaline waters are related to limestone or carboniferous rock while soft acid water comes off granite, old red sandstone, quartzite, schist and gneiss. The former are generally referred to as limestone rivers. The latter as moorland or 'bog' rivers. Fortunately, for the trout fisher, most of the central part of the country is of carboniferous limestone or related rocks and only the mountainous areas around the coast are of granite and other 'less desirable' rock (see map opposite). Limestone is associated with fertile land, good cattle and horses. The rivers that traverse such land hold equally good-quality trout. Conversely, swift fast-flowing streams and rivers rushing down the sides and through valleys surrounded by rocky mountains are rarely worth fishing and the trout fisher heads for the richer waters that meander around the more fertile drumlin hills and across the flat central plain.

But even then, the observant wet fly fisher has to be knowledgeable and discriminating in his choice of a wet fly river. Ideally, for the beginner at any rate, it should not be intimidating: big, deep and fast flowing. Rather it is much better to choose a tributary of one of the major rivers, one with a good grade and flow with lots of broken water and, because it is a tributary, it's unlikely to be too deep. For the beginner, it is difficult to get the flies down to the trout's level in deep water and trout can be notoriously lazy and unco-operative at times, wanting their dinner to be presented right in front of them every time. This isn't easy to do on a big river and hence better sport may be found on a tributary where everything is more intimate and it is possible to fish every inch of the fish-holding water. More important, it is also easier to spot the features mentioned above where trout will be holding up. These are what we call 'lies'.

Trout are creatures of the temperate zones of this world and along with everyone who lives in these parts, they don't like extremes of temperature. They normally feed by sight and have definite periods when they feed – and times too when they can be maddeningly uninterested, even when food is in plentiful supply. But if food is in short supply, they will often take anything that comes their way. These are facts that the river fisher must learn. The fishing is never good if the weather is too hot or too cold, too bright or too dark, too low, or in a raging flood. So it is good to learn and remember when it is likely to be good, like for instance, when the river is clearing and dropping back to a normal level after a flood. Anglers often talk of 'good fishing conditions'. Part of the challenge is learning what these are and consequently being at the river and fishing at the right time.

EQUIPMENT

It is pointless making the journey to the river if you are not equipped for the job. There are certain basic requirements, so let's start at the feet and work up. Normally, we can't fish a river without getting our feet wet. By and large, wellies are useless, a sure way of getting your feet wet. Thigh waders are a minimum requirement and if you really want to get the most out of it, invest in chest waders. In spring, warm socks, layers of warm clothes, a hat or peaked cap and glasses (for eye protection) are the next requirement. For comfort and safety in wading, a wading staff is a wonderful support and a life jacket or buoyancy aid can provide extra warmth and even be a life saver. To make the most of a river, it is generally necessary to wade at least part of it and sometimes most of it if there is a lot of bankside cover.

Depending on the river to be fished, the rod will vary from 8–10 feet and be matched to an AFTM 4 or 5 line. I don't use a sinking line. Hence the choice is between a floating line – for low water conditions and summer fishing – a sink-tip line for medium water or cold conditions in spring, and a sink-tip with a sinking leader attached for high water in spring. With this combination of lines and a variety of leaders of differing sinking rates, it is possible to fish at the appropriate depth on most rivers. Other requirements are a tackle bag or fishing vest, a fly box, small scissors,

RETURNING YOUR TROUT TO THE WATER (an enlightened approach in my view). Be sure to handle it with utmost care and only keep it out of the water for the minimum of time.

forceps for removing the fly from a deeply hooked trout, a spool of 4lb monofilament and a jar of a Fuller's earth based sinkant for removing the shine and sinking the leader.

A small landing net is useful but in time the beginner will learn how to land a trout with a wet hand. And finally, a small priest for knocking the fish briskly on the head. Hopefully, it will not be used too often and most of your trout will be returned alive and well to the water to be caught another day. If you decide to take one home, it is as well to dispatch it quickly and humanely with the proper tool for the job.

The length of the leader is usually 9–10 feet and not longer than 10 and that will include the butt piece. It can be tapered for easier presentation, 2ft of 10lb, 2ft of 6lb and the rest – including the dropper or two droppers, if that's your choice, of 4–6 lb nylon. Beginners often start with just one dropper and a point fly.

CHOOSING WET FLIES

Wet flies are legion. In the early season with little or no insect life about, my own rule of thumb is that good presentation and knowing how the fly works underwater is far more important than which pattern it is. I use only a few patterns. At the top of my list is a Silver Spider (silver body and two turns of black hen hackle), size 12–16, a Hare's Ear or Hare's Ear Nymph and a Stick Fly. After that you can take your pick. It can be anything from a Greenwell's Glory, or Bibio to a Peter Ross or a Zulu. They will all catch a trout on their day.

Why does the trout take a fly? The question is as old as the sport of flyfishing. As far as I can see, there are three basic motivations: (1) hunger, (2) curiosity, (3) aggression. Of these three, the former (hunger) is likely to be most important. Like every other creature on this earth, trout get hungry and when they do, they must eat. Their food is the insects, crustaceans and small fish they find around them. Now, trout mainly search out their food by sight, so the kind of eye they have and how they see is important. The trout's eye is adapted to water and differs from ours. According to the experts, the trout has quite good vision, and it sees particularly well in low light conditions. The trout also has a wide field of vision and can see in virtually every direction at the same time. It can see and distinguish colours, particularly red, orange and yellow. They also react to contrasting shades and stripes.

But, living as they do in a different medium from us and with the artificial fly being frequently presented on the edge of that medium – on, or just below, the water surface which itself may be broken and rippled – it follows that a trout's vision can be distorted. Otherwise, why should it ever accept a concoction of fur, feather and tinsel wrapped around a hook in the belief that it is a living organism? It is my belief that if the shape, size and tone or colour of a fly approximates to something that it is accustomed to seeing in a given situation, it may well investigate it by taking it into its mouth and trying to eat it.

Hence, depending on the fishing conditions, we fish flies that we call 'deceivers' (Claret & Mallard, Sooty Olive, Connemara Black); 'attractors' (Dunkeld, Silver Invicta, Peter Ross); or 'imitative patterns' (artificial nymphs, pupa imitations and various Mayfly patterns). All of them will catch fish on their day and some will work much better than others in particular situations. Therein lies the art of flyfishing.

CASTING THE WET FLY

Good fly presentation is what flyfishing is all about, even wet flyfishing. This means that the angler has to be able to cast well and have good line control. To tackle a river effectively and deal with the various obstructions and challenges, it is not enough to be able to overhead cast only. This limits the possibilities too much. One has to be able to roll cast, switch cast and double switch cast, depending on the situation, to take care of all eventu-

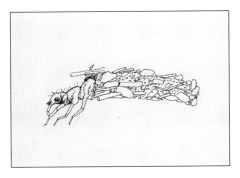
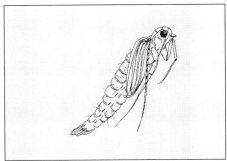
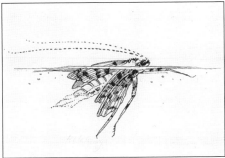

HATCHING STAGES OF THE SEDGE. River trout will eat sedges at each of these stages. Clockwise from top left: cased caddis, pupa, adult fly and the drowning fly.

alities. We must be able to get the fly to where the trout can see it, in spite of bankside bushes and obstructions. Equally, being equipped for wading is so important. A river can be fished so much more effectively when wading, unless of course the banks are level and entirely free of obstructions. This is rarely the case. Anyway, I always consider that the obstructions make the business of fishing so much more challenging and interesting.

FLY PRESENTATION

With the line selected and on the rod and the flies decided upon and tied on securely with a well tied tucked half blood knot, it is time to approach the top of a stream or turbulent run, preferably between 1½ and 2½ feet deep. The approach should be cautious. Trout may be gullible but they are not stupid. They are wild creatures and take fright easily. So move slowly along the bank, keep well back if possible, walk lightly particularly on gravel and, above all, don't arrive in the water with a 'spla-a-ash' like an overturned juggernaut and expect to catch trout.

Fishing wet fly downstream and across, the cast is usually made at 45 degrees across the river towards the far bank. The flies sink and the water begins to sweep them down and across towards your bank. But this is not good enough. We mustn't let the water dictate and sweep them around at an unnaturally fast speed. The angler must learn to control how they move. They must not drag too fast nor skate on the surface. Rather, they should be carried along at about the same speed as the current. Your flies should have the appearance of some hapless underwater creature that has lost its

THE INCREDIBLE KELLY KETTLE, so much a part of the Irish fishing scene. A handful of dry twigs and a scoop of local water will provide tea for several anglers.

A typical early season river trout caught on the wet fly dropper. Whatever its size the first trout of the season is always a happy event. Later in the year it may get a little plumper and perhaps even come to the dry fly.

footing and is being carried away downstream. The movement and speed of the flies' progress is controlled by frequent 'mending' of the line. This is an oval movement of the rod tip which throws the belly of the line upstream. The initial mend is usually the biggest one and thereafter smaller mends are made till the line is directly downstream and the leader makes its final quick dash 'around the corner'. Then take a step forward, make another cast and fish it through as before, ever vigilant to how the flies are moving relative to the water. Soon you discover that there is more to wet flyfishing than 'chuck and chance it'. A well presented fly usually gets a response.

Takes to the wet fly are sudden affairs. Often without warning or any sign of a surface movement, they snatch the fly. The fish may be on for a while and, just when you think he is yours, the hook comes away, the line slackens sickeningly and the trout is gone.

But once hooked, up goes the rod and the fish is played against its spring. If it wants to run, let it run and get the line on to the reel. It's easier to play a good trout off the reel. If it runs towards an obstruction, lay the rod to one side and the side strain is usually enough to effect a change of direction and away from danger. When it begins to weaken and starts wallowing at the surface, draw it carefully over the rim of the net and lift it clear of the water. If the trout is being released again, hold it in the water using the mesh of the net to improve the grip. Remove the hook quickly, face the trout upstream and when it has recovered, let it go.

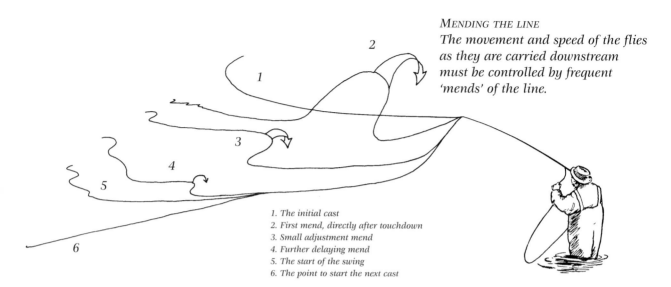

MENDING THE LINE
The movement and speed of the flies as they are carried downstream must be controlled by frequent 'mends' of the line.

1. *The initial cast*
2. *First mend, directly after touchdown*
3. *Small adjustment mend*
4. *Further delaying mend*
5. *The start of the swing*
6. *The point to start the next cast*

UPSTREAM NYMPH

For anyone who hasn't actually seen the upstream nymph method of fishing, it is difficult to persuade them to try it by description alone. Yet it is well worth learning, for it is extraordinarily effective. Having fished a river downstream as far as you can go, it is then possible to turn around and fish back up again with a weighted nymph.

One difference between this and wet flyfishing down and across is that when the angler becomes proficient at spotting the takes, more trout are hooked and fewer lost because the hook is being pulled back into the mouth rather than forward and out of it when you strike.

The ideal rod for fishing the nymph is one of about 9½ feet long with a floating line – and it must float right down to its very tip. The leader can be 9 or 10 ft long with the butt part greased. The pattern of nymph is not, in most cases, all that important. I usually choose either a Pheasant Tail or a Hare's Ear. Generally, they should be weighted according to the depth and speed of the water. Nymph fishing was first publicised as a legitimate angling technique by G.E.M. Skues and it was developed further by the English river keeper, Frank Sawyer. I learned it from Mike Weaver, another Englishman with remarkable skills for fishing both the nymph and the dry fly. The first skill in nymph fishing is to be able to pick out the likely places where trout might lie in a stream. The nymph is then cast accurately upstream with a tuck cast and far enough ahead to take account of current and depth and ensure it has sunk to the level of the trout by the time it reaches the quarry. The flyline is retrieved at the same speed as the water. This requires good hand-eye co-ordination, but this will come with practice. The angler develops a facility to watch the end of the line and the belly of the line near the rod tip – both at the same time. The end of the flyline and the leader must be watched carefully for the slightest sign of it checking, dipping or sliding slightly sideways. The rod is generally held to the side and at the first indication of a take, the angler strikes smartly. Initially it is easy to be misled by the nymph touching the bottom or catching up in underwater vegetation but, with practice, it becomes easier to distinguish a take from a snag. The take is easy to spot. It is always quick and positive whereas a snag causes a slow drag.

For both wet fly and nymph fishing, dedication and practice hones the skills. The powers of observation become more acute with every successive outing. More and more, the angler learns to find and fish the productive water.

CASTING THE NYMPH UPSTREAM Always aim to drop your nymph well above the position in which the fish is lying, allowing the nymph time to sink to the fish's depth.

Direction of current

FAVOURITE WET FLIES FOR THE RIVER

Every angler has his own favourite flies. This will be due to the success they have brought to you and the happy memories they conjure up of wonderful days by the river or on the lough when fortune smiled and bestowed favours that are etched deeply in the mind. Fortune's favours are not earned cheaply in flyfishing. They are the rewards of skill, care and meticulous preparation and this applies equally to the flies we use. We select them because, after a lot of experience, we have confidence in them. I am convinced that the angler whose mind is at ease with the fly he is using will always fish better and catch more fish. Of course, we all have our own favourites, and I list some of mine here simply to give encouragement and to boost the confidence of others less experienced. Before long every angler will have his own favourite patterns – simple, functional and effective ones.

SILVER SPIDER

Hook: Size 12–16
Tying silk: Black
Body: Flat silver tinsel
Rib (optional): Fine silver wire
Hackle: One and a half or two turns (maximum) of natural black hen.

Flies don't come much more simple, nor effective, than this one. I remember catching forty trout on it in one session above and below a bridge on the Curry River and those were not the only trout it took that day either. It can be fished either on the point – my first choice – or the dropper. The smaller sizes (14 and 16) can be surprisingly effective. Fish it with confidence, particularly early in the season, and again in the autumn.

GOLD RIBBED HARE'S EAR NYMPH

Hook: Size 12–14
Tying silk: Fawn or brown
Rib: Fine flat or oval gold tinsel

Tail: Fibres of guard hair from a hare's mask
Body: Hare's ear fur
Thorax: Dark hare's ear fur, built up
Legs: Under part of the thorax well picked out with dubbing brush or needle

The GRHE nymph can be used in all sorts of situations: from imitating nymphs at the surface to various crustacea on the bottom. It is probably one of the most effective nymphs an angler can use and it does not have to look tidy, neat or well tied. It can be tied on either straight shank or 'grub' hooks and can be fished weighted or unweighted. It looks so drab and inconspicuous in the fly box that you can easily pass over it but the trout won't miss it and they will take it with confidence. It has given rise to a number of variants.

The most important and useful of thpese is the addition of a gold bead head, especially good for upstream nymphing. Another excellent variant is a gold head with a partridge (grey or brown) hackle wound behind it.

WET & DRY FLIES FOR THE RIVER
Top row (Dry) Klinkhämer, Parachute Olive, CDC & Elk
2nd row (Dry) Yellow CDC, Green Peter, CDC Smut
3rd row (Wet) Silver Spider, Partridge & Orange, Gold-Ribbed Hare's Ear nymph
Bottom row (Wet) Greenwell's Glory, Stick Fly

STICK FLY

Hook: Size 8–10 long shank
Tying silk: Yellow
Rib: Copper wire
Underbody: Fine lead or copper wire
Tail: Four fibres of peacock herl
Body: Bronze peacock herl
Hackle: Two turns of ginger hen
Head: Yellow wool or goldhead bead
The cased caddis (or stick fly) is the larva of one of the many sedges that build a house or case of sand and vegetation around them to camouflage them against predators – trout included. The larva inside are especially succulent and attractive to big trout, especially early in the season when there is little else available by way of food. They are most plentiful in limestone rivers with stony bottoms. Fish the artificial on a sink-tip line or a sinking braided leader close to the bottom, allowing it to trundle around in the current.

GREENWELL'S GLORY

Hook: Size 12–16
Rib: Gold wire
Tail: Fibres of Greenwell or Coch-y-bonddu hackle
Body: Primrose tying silk pulled through brown cobblers' wax
Hackle: Greenwell or Coch-y-bonddu hen
Wing: Starling wing slips
This is a great top dropper pattern in different sizes. It can be used all through the season when the various olives are hatching on the river. The original pattern was tied with a wing but nowadays many anglers prefer to omit the wing and tie it as a spider pattern using two turns of Greenwell's hen hackle. The shade of the body can also vary and this can be achieved by using black tying silk over-laid with either primrose or yellow floss silk.

PARTRIDGE AND ORANGE

Hook: Size 14 and 16
Tying silk: Orange
Rib: Gold wire or fine oval gold tinsel
Body: Orange floss
Hackle: Brown partridge
The Partridge and Orange is one of those flies which can take a trout when nothing else will work. It's effective right through the season especially on the limestone rivers. For best results, keep the body slim and don't overdress with hackle.

WET FLY FISHING DOWNSTREAM on a typical peaty river in Western Ireland. Keeping a low profile on the bank is always a good idea, whether you are fishing wet or dry fly.

2

Fishing the Dry Fly
for River Trout

I think we have all approached dry fly fishing with a certain amount of trepidation. Even in a country like Ireland with a small angling press and even scarcer history of angling literature, somehow the word got around that dry fly fishing was difficult, both to learn and to practice. Dry fly fishing was regarded as some kind of higher art form, surrounded by mystery. Certainly there was a great lack of practical information about the basic requirements. Equipment was poor, casting techniques often left a lot to be desired and the possiblility of being seen and critised by one's peers discouraged many. As a result anglers shied away from it. Another factor in the creation of the mystery was the scarcity of basic information about fly life and the life cycle of river insects. The last straw for many was to be presented with a scholarly work on entomology fit for a professor. The confusion that a diet of olives, duns and spinners, imagos and sub-imagos, green drakes and gnats can cause, not to mention 'ephemeroptera, tricoptera and plecoptera', was enough to give anyone a severe and possibly terminal bout of dry fly indigestion. What it all amounted to was that the few who fished the dry fly enjoyed themselves but they did not give away many of its secrets. For the rest, it was difficult to break into the dry fly circle.

But when all the mystery is peeled away, dry fly fishing is as easy to learn as any other kind – and it's fascinating. This probably explains why a small band of fishermen travel from all parts of the world every year to fish the dry fly on some of our rivers, not to mention of course the increasing number of Irish dry fly enthusiasts. You have only to walk along the banks of any Midland river in the month of May or June to realise just how many have discovered the secret.

The basic requirement for dry fly fishing is to find a rising fish, or one that can be persuaded to rise. He is not difficult to spot because he gives away his presence by making rings on the surface of the water as he feeds on floating insects. Anyone can see them on calm pools and, with a minimum of practice, they can be spotted on moving water as well. The angler then selects a fly that floats and casts it in front of the rising trout without frightening him. The trout takes the fly on its next rise and the angler hooks, plays and lands it. The description may be a little oversimplified but that, in essence, is what happens. Sometimes it will work, sometimes it doesn't. There is nothing very difficult about it. There are no rules or certainties, for it is not an exact science. It is just an angler bent on fooling a trout into taking a concoction of feathers and furs tied on a hook which has created the illusion that it is a real insect.

FINDING A DRY FLY RIVER

The geology of the countryside determines the kind of river that flows over it. By 'kind of river' in this context we mean whether it is or is not good for dry fly fishing. Basically, this is determined by the productivity of a river or stream. This in turn depends on whether the water chemistry is alkaline, neutral or acid. Acid streams and rivers are mainly found around the coast flowing swiftly off the mountains. They have beds of granite or some such hard rock. Insect life is scarce and the trout are small. Our typical dry fly river is found where the landscape is more productive. It may be hilly or it may be flat, cultivated, in pasture or even bogland, but you will invariably find that the underlying geological formation is carboniferous limestone or a similar soft rock (see map on page 24). This is the predominant rock formation of the central plain of Ireland and hence our landscape is criss-crossed with dry fly rivers of varying quality from the Upper Bann and Lagan in the North to the Suir and Bandon in the South and from the Boyne and Liffey in the East to the Robe and Clare in the West.

Mayfly

Sedge

Midge

    Of course, the underlying rock may vary and with it the topographical characteristics of the countryside, creating hugely varying aquatic environments and flow regimes. But broadly speaking, it is here we find what we call our limestone streams and rivers that still have the potential to produce a wealth of dry fly fishing. They vary in size and character from narrow streams to broad, placid flowing rivers. Some are wonderfully natural and unspoiled by human activity, others have been drained and some have been expensively rehabilitated. The rest have been allowed to recover naturally from damaging arterial drainage works and some are surprisingly good. Nearly all of them hold trout from ½ to 3lbs or 4lbs and occasionally a whopper of 6lbs, 8lbs or even 10lbs is landed.

Beetle

Drone fly

TYPES OF WATER

There are different 'types of water' to be found throughout a river and those favoured by the dry fly fisher are the runs, glides, flats and pools. Each type presents its own challenges for each has its own particular speed of current, bottom type and bankside character.

FLY LIFE

The first requirement of a dry fly river is an abundance of fly life to lure the trout to the surface. A basic knowledge of the more important species that hatch on the river is essential for the dry fly angler, as is the time of day and season in which these insects emerge and lay their eggs. Don't expect to find every species on every river, because you won't. A few terrestrial insects like beetles and caterpillars get blown on to the water from time to time and we should be familiar with them too. It must be remembered that trout have neither calendars nor watches and neither have insects. They don't abide by rigid rules and hence the best I can do is give broad guidelines that I hope will apply in average situations.

FLY HATCHES IN IRELAND

Blue-winged olive

There is rarely an opportunity to fish a dry fly in early March (except maybe on the River Dodder in Dublin) but at the end of March, depending on temperature and weather conditions, large dark olives appear and continue into April together with iron blue duns, medium olives and small dark olives. The medium olives and small dark olives continue into May and sometimes into June.

Hawthorn fly

May and June are two very productive months with various small sedges including grey flags, mayflies, pale wateries, pale evening duns, yellow evening duns, yellow may duns, purple duns, caenis, various midges and reed smuts. The two most important terrestrials at this time are the hawthorn and the black gnat (which is not unlike the reed smut).

Black gnat

In July, various sedges (both small and big) are important, as are blue-winged olives (and their spinner, the sherry spinner), pale wateries, pale evening duns, yellow may duns, small dark olives, black gnats, various midges, reed smuts and ants (both red and black).

Flying ant

In August, the variety of available species begins to diminish and blue-winged olives, pale evening duns and various sedges and midges are still important. The same list applies in September and to it large dark olives and iron blue duns can be added.

THE DAILY HATCH TIMES

The times of day in which trout will take the dry fly will vary throughout the season. This reflects the activity of the more important flies – when they emerge, hatch out, return to the water to lay their eggs, or simply get blown on to it.

◎ In late March and early April, the hatch usually occurs from noon till 3pm. Don't break for lunch!
◎ From mid-April to mid-May, the best of the fishing is likely to be from noon till about 3pm and in the early evening.
◎ From mid-May to mid-June, one is likely to witness surface activity from early morning till dark.
◎ From mid-June till the end of August, day time fishing can be patchy but very good in the evenings till dark.
◎ In September, the best rises occur during the day. The evenings can turn

a trifle chilly and this often reduces insect activity.

The above is but a general guide to what happens. Fishing conditions and regional variations ensure that no two days and no two rivers, even adjoining ones, are ever the same. One river may be devoid of fly life or rising trout and yet a neighbouring stream can be alive with trout at the same time. It is just one of the facts of life with which the dry fly fisher has to come to terms.

CHOOSING THE RIGHT FLY

Trout take up positions in a river and wait for the current to carry the flies down to them. With a little practice and familiarisation on your own river, you soon learn to spot the productive stretches, the good lies and even where the biggest trout hang out. Once a trout has been spotted feeding, the next task is to ascertain the fly it is taking. It will generally fall into one of four broad categories:

1. UPWINGED FLIES

(1) upwinged flies (and here it can be either a dun or a spinner)
(2) sedges
(3) black gnats or midges or
(4) a terrestrial

These are broad categories. They will vary by species, size, shape and colour. With a little practice, these features are easy enough to spot. What is important is not how we see the fly but how it appears to the trout from below. Trout see things differently to us and they don't have time to put things under a microscope to determine species, sex, etc. Nor has man the capability of tying a fly so precisely that it becomes an exact imitation – indistinguishable from the natural. The best the angler can hope for is to create an illusion for the trout which gives the impression that it is something which is good to eat and does not look out of place with the rest of the meal which he is presently enjoying. With a little basic angling entomology, you should have little difficulty in identifying the order to which a fly belongs and then selecting an artificial to match it for size, shape and shade of colour. It would be quite impossible to list all the dry fly patterns that are available. Their numbers would fill several fly tying dictionaries. On most rivers, all that is needed is a few good general patterns for each order of flies in a range of sizes: at least that has been my experience. Rarely is it necessary to come close to exact imitation of the natural insect. Only when fishing pressure is exceptionally heavy and the trout become educated or in a prolific hatch when the trout may home in on just one particular species – only then might exact imitation be required. I no longer find it necessary to take several boxes of flies to the river. A small selection to suit water type and insects present (Sedge, Olive or Black Gnat) is generally adequate. Some of my personal favourites are: Adams, Iron Blue, Black Gnat, Mosely Mayfly, Spent Gnat, CDC Midge (in various shades), Parachute Olive, Kite's Imperial, Comparadun, Lunn's

2. ROOF-WINGED FLIE

3. FLAT-WINGED FLIES

4. TERRESTRIALS

44

Particular, Pheasant Tail, Pale Watery, Elk Hair Caddis, De Vaux Sedge, Ethafoam Sedge and (never be without it) a Klinkhämer Special. Too often when fishing to rising trout, anglers think that by not having the 'right fly', they might as well quit. Not true! A wide range of imitations will catch a feeding trout. There are many reasons why a trout may refuse a fly. It may be too big. Maybe it isn't presented accurately and the trout doesn't see it. It might be water logged. The leader may be too thick or, all too often, it is dragging. How often have we seen two or three different anglers succeed with entirely different patterns fishing the same hatch. Try to be prepared in advance and always have some small flies – sizes 16–20 – handy.

RODS, LINES AND LEADERS FOR RIVERS

It pays to choose a dry fly rod well. It will be your friend and ally. My preference is for a middle-to-tip, or progressive, action carbon fibre rod. Length depends on the size of river I'm fishing and it can range from 7 feet upwards, but never more than 9 feet. A shorter rod is essential on the tree-lined streams but for most other rivers, an eight or eight and a half foot rod is adequate.

Regarding flylines, an AFTM No.5 floating line is about right, particularly for the beginner who may have problems trying to cast a lighter line.

There are various combinations of leaders on the market but for the dry fly, after trying them all, I prefer the modern tapered monofilament leaders. It virtually eliminates knots and turns over well. Attach it to the line by inserting a needle in the end of the line, withdraw it and insert the butt of the leader. Scuff about an inch of the butt with emery paper. Apply a little waterproof glue and pull it gently into the flyline. It gives a wonderfully smooth connection. Alternatively, use a needle knot.

The length of your leader will be determined by the location and fishing conditions. Nine foot is minimum and for a competent caster, and it can be as long as 12 feet when conditions are calm and the banks allow easy backcasting.

Leaders become short through changing flies and chopping off pieces and it may be necessary to add to its length. This piece is usually about three foot long and attached to the leader with a four-turn water knot or a grinner knot. This final length of monofilament is called the tippet and, depending on the fishing conditions and the average size of the trout, the breaking strain can vary from 1lb to 4lb, and occasionally even 6lb.

CONSTRUCTION OF THE DRY FLY LEADER

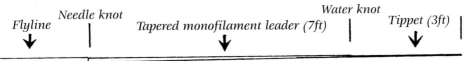

Flyline   Needle knot   Tapered monofilament leader (7ft)   Water knot   Tippet (3ft)

CASTING AND FLY PRESENTATION

We are now deeply enough into the subject to consider what exactly the dry fly fisher has to do, for such art as there is in dry fly fishing has to do with choosing the right fly and fly presentation. The rudiments of dry fly presentation have been distilled to their essence by generations of anglers and it goes something like this. In a nutshell, fishing the dry fly is about selecting the correct imitation and presenting it properly. First you find a trout that is feeding on surface insects. Then select an artificial fly that matches the insect as closely as possible in terms of shape, size and colour. Take care not to disturb the trout as you approach and place the fly accurately and lightly on the water a yard or two in front of the trout so that it floats without drag. Fishing the Sedge can sometimes be an exception to this rule, but for the others they must not drag unnaturally.

Good dry fly presentation is fundamentally rooted in fly casting. How good a dry fly fisher you are has nothing to do with how far you can cast a fly but has a lot to do with how accurately and lightly you can present the fly. I'm frequently amazed at so many anglers' preoccupation with achieving 'distance' and how little consideration is given to exactly where the fly ends up. I keep reminding beginners that it counts for naught if the fly is made of the finest silk and hackles and dressed on gold-plated hooks if it does not land in the trout's window of vision. With a wet fly, we can swing it across the current and search the water. A dry fly, that does not fall exactly on the target will not be seen by the trout. I am confident that many more dry flies are 'refused' by trout because they have not been seen rather than because the trout did not like the look of them.

We can learn a lot about fly casting accuracy from shooting instructors, for accuracy in dry fly fishing is just as critical as it is in shooting. Shooters use one eye – their master eye – to look down the barrel of the gun at the target. They are careful too about body posture and how they hold the gun. The same concept applies to fly casting. The dry fly cast calls for absolute accuracy. Begin by standing with the right foot forward. (Left-handed anglers place the left foot forward). Lean slightly forward. Tuck the elbow close in to the body and lift the rod hand up in front of the face and as you make the back cast, rock back on the left foot. A good dry fly cast involves not just good hand-eye co-ordination but harmonious interaction throughout your whole body. Your rod should sweep back in as straight a vertical plane as possible and pass close by your cheek or better still, tilt back directly over the head. In the forward cast, lean forward

Direction of current

and complete the cast with the rod vertically in front of the right eye, so that you are sighting over it at the rise as you complete the forward cast. This ensures that you do not distort your aim as you target a rising trout. If you adopt any other stance and hold the rod away from the face, you cannot see what is really happening because you are sighting the rise at an angle to the rod. As a consequence your fly may land at a point which was not intended. Always remember that time-honoured maxim in dry fly fishing: 'A rising trout gives you one good chance – the first one'. So try and make the first cast count. One mistake and your trout will be on his guard for the next one.

TACTICS ON THE RIVER BANK

Once you have spotted a rising trout and selected the fly, the next thought should be about how to approach it. The trout must not see the angler. Keep well back from the bank, move slowly and quietly, keep low and get downstream of the fish. Trout have a blind spot and it is possible to approach a trout from behind to within five or six yards without being seen. So you approach from behind either along the bank or wading. Get as close as possible. This is all about accuracy and good presentation. The majority of trout are caught on dry fly casts of between six and twelve yards. The longer the cast, the greater the margin for error. Take care that there is room for the back cast and no danger of snagging. If possible, take up a position a little to the left or right rather than directly behind. This ensures that the trout sees only the fly and not the leader as it drifts over. It is now time to make the cast. A couple of quick false casts gets the line moving. Now another problem becomes immediately apparent. How to measure the exact length of line? This comes with practice and as a famous golfer once remarked – 'The more I practice, the luckier I become.' Here are two tips. Firstly, do not measure the distance to the trout by repeated false casting till you think the fly is over it. The trout is likely to spot the fly and leader whizzing over its head and be frightened. Do the false casting to one side. Secondly, if you are to make a mistake, make it short. Too long a cast will 'line' the trout and put it down. A short cast drifts harmlessly downstream. It can be picked up, an extra yard of line extended and cast again.

Trout often adopt a rhythm when rising. For example, they may rise

Looking down the fly rod helps you to cast with the accuracy and precision that is essential in dry fly fishing

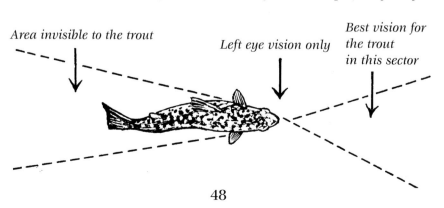

Area invisible to the trout

Left eye vision only

Best vision for the trout in this sector

THE TROUT'S AREA OF VISION

The Principal Upwinged Flies on Irish Rivers

Common name of natural fly	Distinguishing features of dun	Distribution and location	Season	Time of emergence	Artificial wet fly or nymph	Artificial dun	Artificial spinner
March brown *R. haarupi*	Mottled wings, brown olive body, 2 tails	Stony, acid rivers	March, April, May	During the day	March Brown Partridge & Orange Size 12-14	March Brown Size 12-14	Pheasant Tail Spinner Size 12-14
Large dark olive *B. rhodani*	Grey wings, olive-grey body, 2 tails	Both limestone and acid rivers	April/September	Mid-day to early afternoon	GRHE Red Spinner Greenwell's Glory Size 12	Adams Beacon Beige GRHE Klinkhämer Greenwell's Glory Size 12	Red Spinner (wet)
Medium olive *B. tenax*	Smaller and paler than Large dark olive, 2 tails	As above, very widespread	April-Sept Peaks in May-June	Mid-day and afternoon	GRHE Size 14-16	(as above) Size 14	Lunn's Particular (in evening) Size 14-16
Iron blue *B. pumilus*	Small, dark brown appearance (even black) 2 tails	Limestone and acid rivers	April-Sept, but peaks in May	Mid-day	Iron Blue Dun (wet) Hatching Iron Blue Size 14-16	Iron Blue Dun Size 16-18	Houghton Ruby Jenny Spinner Size 16-18
Mayfly *E. danica*	By far the biggest upwinged fly, 3 tails	Limestone and moderately acid rivers	Mid-May to mid-June and occasionally in August	10.30am - mid-day and in the afternoon	Mayfly Nymph Large GRHE nymph Wet Mayfly Size 8-10	Mosely Mayfly Humpy (red & yellow) Yellow Wulff Klinkhämer Size 8-12	Grey Wulff Spent Gnat Royal Wulff Size 8-10
Claret dun *L. vespertina*	Very dark black-claret body, 3 tails	Acid moorland rivers	May, June, July	During the day	Small Claret & Mallard Size 14-16	Claret Dun Size 14-16	Pheasant Tail Spinner Size 14-16
Pale watery *C. luteolum*	Pale grey wings and pale olive body, 2 tails	Limestone rivers	May to September	During the day in May & June Evenings later	–	Grey Duster CDC & pale olive body Pale parachute olive Comparadun Size 14-18	Tup's Indispensable Lunn's Particular Size 14-16
Yellow may dun (mis-named Yellow Sally) *H. sulphurea*	Bright yellow body, 2 tails	Slow flowing limestone rivers	Late May, June & July	During the day and early evening	–	Yellow May Dun Size 14-18	Yellow May Spinner Size 14-18
Yellow evening dun *E. notata*	Yellowish wings, yellow body and 3 tails	Fast water on limestone rivers eg. Liffey, Boyne	May, June, July	Afternoon and early evening	–	Yellow May Dun Pale Parachute Olive Small Comparadun Size 14-16	Yellow May Yellow Evening Dun spinner Size 14-16
Purple dun *P. cincta*	Dark grey wings brown-purple body, 3 tails	Some Barrow tributaries	May to August	During the day	–	Purple Dun Large Iron Blue Dun Size 12-14	Purple Dun Spinner Size 14-16
Blue-winged olive (BWO) *E. ignita*	Blue-grey wings olive body, 3 tails	Widespread	Mid-May to to September	Day and evening in June-July.	Pheasant Tail size 14-18	Comparadun Orange Parachute BWO, Size 16-18	Sherry Spinner Pheasant Tail Spinner Size 16-18
Caenis *Caenis spp*	White wings, cream body, 3 tails, very small	Widespread	June, July	Morning early evening	Small GRHE Size 18-20	Yellow CDC Size 18-20	Yellow CDC Size 18-20
Small dark olive *B. scambus*	Very small olive, 2 tails	Limestone rivers	June, July, early August	Afternoon/early evening	Tiny GRHE Size 18-20	Kite's Imperial Olive Parachute Comparadun, Size 18-20	Red Spinner Pheasant Tail Spinner Size 18-20

every ten seconds or take every fourth fly that passes overhead. The time lag between rises reflects how deep they are lying, how far up they must swim from their holding position to the surface. Try to estimate the interval so that your fly arrives at the moment you would expect the next rise.

A good dry fly cast is made over the water, not at it. The leader straightens two to three feet over the water and the fly 'drops' on its target. Better still, it floats down like thistledown on a cushion of air. This is especially true of patterns dressed with CDC (cul de canard) hackle.

The next problem the angler has to watch out for is 'drag', the bane of every dry fly fisher. 'Drag' is caused by the line and leader pulling on the fly so that instead of it drifting naturally on the water, it is 'dragged' sideways or downstream. This immediately alerts the trout to the fact that it's a phoney fly. Drag is caused by the complex and varying speed of the surface water of a river. The fly sometimes alights on slow moving water and the leader and line on faster water. Anglers have different ways of overcoming it. They include a check cast, an upstream bend in the line or simply wriggling the rod from side to side as soon as it has stopped on the

ABOVE:
Upstream
nymphing on
the Nore. Mike
Weaver, a
master practi-
tioner, in
characteristic
pose: hunched
forward in
anticipation of
the slightest
twitch of the
line which will
indicate a take

forward cast. It's ironic that we spend a lot of time learning to cast a straight line but this is one situation where the line and leader should not be laid out straight. The object here is to give the fly a chance to float over the fish before the current irons out the wiggles in the line and leader and the fly starts to drag.

Spotting a take on time is critical. Wild trout eject an artificial fly quickly. The angle of light on the water can be favourable or a hindrance depending on the location, the season and even the time of day. The situation can be improved by varying the angle of approach. For instance, it is always easier to spot a take in the shadow of a tree or bush than against the glare of direct light – except, of course, in the evening twilight. In certain situations wearing polarised glasses can be a disadvantage and result in a late strike and missed takes.

Next comes the moment you have been waiting for. A trout takes your fly! What next? You strike and set the hook. Correct timing of the strike is critical and, quite simply, you will never get it right all the time. There are broad guidelines like strike small trout quickly and delay with a big trout. Fast water demands a quick reaction. There are no hard and fast rules. Sometimes inexplicably, you miss trout after trout with both quick and slow strikes despite the fly being sucked under. On other occasions, you can do no wrong.

When a trout is hooked, keep calm and hold the rod tip aloft. Allow the fish to tire gradually and let it run against the drag of the reel when it desires. Use side strain to direct it away from snags or weed beds. If the inevitable happens and it lodges in thick vegetation, stand directly downstream, put steady strain on the fish, 'twang' the taut line like a fiddle string – and be patient. Eventually many trout are recovered this way. They tire and back out into clear water.

Once again, it is well to remember that there are no hard and fast rules and observation and inventiveness pay dividends. For instance, a Sedge may be fished upstream but if it doesn't get a response, change position, cast downstream and let it drag across the trout's nose. Or, on a calm pool, where trout are patrolling and taking black gnats or spinners, it is much better to spend a little time observing the path a trout takes. Sometimes they cruise around the pool in a big circle.

When the trout is well away, cast the fly on the water and wait. Even flies that don't represent sedges and therefore must not drag can sometimes be cast downstream with lots of slack line, if the situation does not allow for an upstream cast. The challenges and the satisfaction of dry fly fishing on a river are never ending.

FAVOURITE DRY FLIES FOR THE RIVER

I am all too conscious that these are purely *my* favourites. Someone else would most probably make an entirely different choice. When I go to the river I tend to travel light and that extends to my fly selection too. The rivers I fish hold wild brown trout and I find if I have a few patterns in the right size to match the insects I expect will be on the water, I'm satisfied. In the majority of cases we are faced with either a hatch of various olives, sedges or black gnats or reed smut. So if I'm fishing dry, I'm thinking either in terms of an emerger or a high-riding dry fly. These flies have caught a lot of trout for me. The Klinkhammer in particular, dressed in a variety of body tones, thorax and hackle colours solves many a problem. See illustration on page 35.

KLINKHÄMER SPECIAL

Hook: Size 8–16 (Treimco 200R or 2457: Sprite Grub Hook: Kamasan B110 or B100: Ashima F–50 Shrimp/Grub: or Scorpion 31270 living larva hook
Tying silk: Brown
Wing: White polypropylene floating yarn (Lureflash)
Body: Fly-Rite poly dubbing – rusty olive, dark tan, black or other shade of one's choice
Hackle: Brown Metz saddle hackle, light ginger or grizzle
Thorax: Dark claret seal's fur or three strands of bronze peacock herl

Five years ago, I wrote that here was a fly to make all other dry flies redundant. I see no reason to change that view. If anything, its reputation has been enhanced in the meantime. That it is in fact an emerger pattern really does not matter. No other fly comes near it for catching trout in river or lough, on fast streamy water or on a slow shiny glide. For those who like to fish dry fly, here is a fly that can be fished to search the water when there is no hatch and nothing rising. Trout will follow it downstream on the river and take it at the last moment. On the lough, I have seen trout come up and examine it. Then, if you give it a little shake or tweak it, they will engulf it. The basic pattern can be varied to accommodate whatever is on the water – Mayflies, Olives, Buzzers, Sedges or even terrestrials.

I have had a lot of success using the dark claret seal's fur thorax. Also, when tying it, remember to wind sufficient turns of hackle to float the bigger patterns. Five turns is a minimum and I prefer to use a genetic hackle for its floating properties.

It is important that the fly sits properly in the water when being fished. Remember the floatant dressing should be applied only to the hackle. The body of the fly should hang below the surface suspended by the hackle in the surface film. To achieve the correct presentation, wet the abdomen before applying the floatant and hold the moistened abdomen between finger and thumb. A really great fly.

CDC & ELK

Hook: Size 12–16
Tying silk: Brown
Body: CDC feather
Hackle: Trailing fibres of CDC
Wing: Natural elk hair, tanned

There are many good Sedge patterns but I have yet to come across a better one than this for both day time and evening river fishing. Ever since I was given it by Hans Weilenmann at the

Dutch Fly Fair about 1993, it has been my number one Sedge pattern for the river. I've taken some very big trout on it on Lough Sheelin too. The first time I used it was on the river Annalee in early May. I fished it 'on the blind' and took three good trout. That convinced me of its worth. I have never been without it since.

Tying tip: the correct choice of the CDC feather is critical in getting the dressing right as the body and hackle are made from the same feather. If you examine a selection of CDC feathers, you will notice that some are short and stubby, others are quite long and in between there is what I describe as a moon-shaped feather with a distinctive rounded tip. This is the required shape. Tie it in by the tip over the hook point, take the stalk in the hackle pliers and wind the body. Towards the end of this operation, it will be noticed that stray fibres of CDC are beginning to fan out. Continue with another two or three turns and a light, downy hackle is formed. Now tie off the stalk and tie in the wing.

CDC SMUT

Hook: Size 16–22
Body: Fly-Rite ply dubbing, black
Wing: CDC

This is the invention of Andrew Ryan – at least it was he who gave me it – and a right good fly it is too for those situations where trout are smutting on something so small that it is virtually impossible to see.

To tie in the wing, after finishing the body, tie in a small CDC feather by the middle with the top pointing forward in front of the eye. Then double back the tip, secure with a couple of turns of silk and tie off. Finally, cut the wing to the desired length.

YELLOW CDC

Hook: Size 16–22
Tying silk: Brown or primrose
Body: Fly-Rite Pale Watery Yellow (BC549) poly dubbing
Hackle: Cul de canard (CDC)

This simple pattern can represent a range of emerging pale olives and midges. If ever there was a fly designed to land on the water as gently as an angel's kiss, this is it. Rather than fall, it glides down ever so gently. One of its strengths is that trout take it in a wide range of situations, often when they have rejected more traditional dry olive patterns. To create the hackle, tie in a CDC feather by the stalk, wind and tie off, then pull it forward over the eye and cut to length with the scissors.

PARACHUTE OLIVE

Hook: Size 14–18
Tying silk: Pale olive
Tail: Blue dun
Body: Fly-Rite Blue Wing Olive (BC% 40/43) dubbing
Hackle: Blue dun or grizzle
Wing: Grey polypropylene floating yarn (Lureflash)

This is a basic pattern that can be varied to accommodate various emerging olives. It is very effective when blue-winged olives are hatching. It is also a useful searching pattern for when the hatch is sparse and trout are slow to show at the surface.

GREEN PETER

Hook: Size 8–12 Kamasan B170 or B175
Tying silk: Black
Rib: Fine oval gold tinsel
Body: Olive green seal's fur or substitute
Body hackle: Red game
Wing: Four slips of hen pheasant secondary feather tied in flat
Hackle: Red game

3

BROWN TROUT FISHING ON

THE LOUGHS

Lough fishing for trout is widely practiced in Ireland from March to early October. This long season is hardly surprising in a country that is so well endowed with trout loughs – literally thousands of them, both big and small. The quality of the fishing varies too. Some loughs hold only a few trout, others teem with fish. Some – like Corrib, Mask and Sheelin – are world famous. The average fish size can vary too from big healthy two pounders to miserable little runts.

Thousands of anglers go lough fishing in Ireland every year. Mostly they fish from boats. A few prefer fishing from the shore and savour the solitude of wilderness fishing in the mountains. Obviously the latter has its own particular attractions. But the challenges for the flyfisher, from hill lough to lowland lough, are much the same: both involve learning about the best fish-holding areas, the times of local fly hatches and the specific habits of trout in different loughs.

TROUT TYPES IN IRELAND

The trout themselves are worthy of comment, such is their diversity and consequent varying habits. The scientists declare all of our native trout to be one species – *Salmo trutta*. But in reality, matters are not so simple. Certainly, in some loughs, the trout may all appear to look the same. But in others, even the angler can notice striking differences in their shape, colour and markings. While all our loughs hold one species of brown trout, some contain up to four different strains of trout. So, we have brown trout (page 70), gillaroo trout (page 95), sonaghan trout (page 15) and ferox trout. All four of these 'races' of trout are particularly associated with Lough Melvin in Co. Leitrim, but they exist in other lakes like Conn, Mask, Corrib and the Killarney Lakes, all of which have an extraordinary diversity of strains. Gillaroo are spectacularly beautiful with vivid orange-red spots while the sonaghan have a more sombre slate grey appearance with black fins and a slim, streamlined body. It is necessary to be aware of their existence because each strain has differing dietary habits and they inhabit

LEFT
Denis O'Keeffe, one of Lough Sheelin's most experienced boatmen takes to the oars with a fine collection of lough flies at his feet.

THE DUCK FLY
HERALD OF NEW SEASON

The duck fly is the Irish anglers' name for medium-sized black midges (chironomids) that hatch on loughs in the latter half of March and in April. They trigger the first real rise of trout of the season and send out an invitation to flyfishers to cast adrift in search of heading-and-tailing trout in the ripple. Duck flies hatch in clear, moderately deep (up to 15 feet) water with lush vegetation and a silt bottom. Thus, the areas in which they are found are limited and often referred to by anglers as 'duck fly holes' or 'pike holes'. Successful anglers and boatmen memorise the exact location of these hot-spots from year to year.

Trout will congregate in the holes and follow the pupae as they ascend to the surface. Hatches may occur throughout the day. Angling tactics include fishing small traditional wet flies, epoxy pupae and various other pupae and emergers. Lough Corrib is the prime duck fly lough. Others of note include Arrow, Lein, Conn, Mask and Sheelin, while on Lough Ennell, there is a prolific hatch that the trout largely ignore for some strange reason.

different parts of the lake. Brown trout are the most common strain likely to be encountered. Gillaroo live in shallow rocky areas and feed on snails and other crustaceans. Sonaghan inhabit the deep water and feed on plankton and invertebrates and usually only become available to the angler in low light conditions when they follow the rising plankton to the surface. Ferox trout live in the deeps, are fish eaters and unlike the other strains, are only occasionally encountered by the flyfisher. And perhaps more unusual still are the 'dollaghan' which run up the tributaries of Lough Neagh; and the 'croneen' of Lough Derg. Both are deep-bodied fish with large dark spots.

Brown trout are found in all kinds of loughs, lowland limestone loughs, inaccessible ponds and bigger sheets of water high in the mountains – provided certain conditions prevail. The chief determining factors are clean water, inflowing streams that provide adequate spawning and nursery areas for young trout and a plentiful food supply. Trout will always be more plentiful when there are fewer competitors (roach, perch) and predators (pike, cormorants). Depth is a factor too. Trout food flourishes in those areas of loughs that average about nine feet or less and this directly determines stock density.

TROUT STOCKS

The number of trout in a lough is a point of major importance to the angler. The greater the stock density, the better chance the angler has of encoun-

SEDGES

Every river fisher is aware of the significance of sedges (*Trichoptera*), sometimes known as caddisflies. They are part of the staple diet of trout in summer and often bring on a sustained rise both by day and in the evening. The grey flag (*Hydropsyche spp.*) is a case in point.

Lough fishers appear obsessed with the Murrough and the Green Peter almost to the exclusion of the smaller species. This, in my opinion, is a great mistake and I have found lough trout are fond of small sedges and often particularly responsive to small dry artificials. It would appear that while hatches of specific species may be sparse, the combined number of these species all hatching together may be sufficiently high and dense to bring on a rise of trout. If several species are on the water at the same time, they are more important collectively than individually. I have especially noted how big trout will take a size 12 or 14 artificial when great big Green Peters are hatching all around. Useful artificials include Michael Kelly's Small Brown Sedge, CDC & Elk Sedge and Devaux Sedge, in sizes 12 or 14.

tering fish. Stocked lakes hold artificially enhanced populations of takable trout – usually more than nature herself is capable of producing. The limiting factors in the wild loughs have been mentioned above (spawning, predators, competitors, etc.).

Nonetheless, some of our big natural loughs have the potential to hold enormous numbers of trout – for example 500,000 were estimated by fishery scentists to be in Lough Conn in the 1980s.

LOCATING TROUT ON THE LOUGH

But even in situations of high stock density, it must be remembered that trout are not spread evenly throughout the whole lake. They concentrate in those areas where food is most readily available. Finding the big concentrations of trout and getting among them is the first challenge of the angler. You have no chance if you fish barren water and even the most productive

OVERLEAF
The Cusack brothers at Cushlough, budding anglers displaying a typical bag of Lough Mask trout to 4¼lb.

LAKE OLIVES

The lake olive (*Cloeon simile*) hatch occurs in the months of April, May and September in small limestone loughs and in sheltered bays and

inlets on the bigger loughs. The hatch, which usually occurs in the morning and mid-afternoon, can bring on a spectacular rise of trout, recognisable by characteristic splashing. Fish 'on the lake olives' can be notoriously difficult to catch, particularly on wet flies. In recent years, anglers report much greater success fishing nymphs, dry flies and especially emerger patterns based on the Greenwell's Glory or CDC & Hare's Ear.

fisheries have lots of water that is virtually devoid of fish. Trout follow the food, and the feeding areas can vary by the season, even by the week. Some areas tend always to hold fish. Others are invariably useless. Local knowledge is the key and boatmen and anglers who fish a lough regularly have it in abundance. After that, angling maps can be a help. Observation and being aware of what is happening around is always important. A group of boats in a particular area can be a tell tale sign and swooping gulls can mean a localised hatch of fly, with both trout and birds competing for emerging flies. A knowledge of the lough bottom contours only comes with experience, or the assistance of someone experienced on the water. They are of immense value in locating trout-holding areas, sometimes referred to as 'shallows' on the bigger loughs.

TYPES OF LOUGH

The topography and geological structure of the countryside in which a lough is situated largely determines the chemical make-up of the water and the size and quality of the trout as well as the numbers that are present. Just as the surrounding landscape can vary from rich pastures and tillage crops on the one hand to bare mountain and acid bog land on the other, so too does the productivity of its loughs. It is basically determined by the underlying rock strata. Hence we have rich loughs and poor loughs, loughs with stocks of large trout and those that contain only tiny trout. The limestone loughs in the central plain of the country hold big fast-growing trout. Mountain and moorland loughs with a low pH value have only small trout and in between, there is a whole range of values and types of water. The diversity is enormous and fascinating, from rich, well known waters like Sheelin and Carra, through Melvin and Lein, to the hill loughs of Donegal and Sligo, Mayo and Kerry, to mention but a few – all beckoning and challenging the angler to have a go.

BROWN TROUT FISHING FROM BANK AND FROM BOAT

Depending on the nature of the shoreline and the size of the water, the lough may be fished either from the shore or from a boat. Bank fishing can be productive and is normally practised on mountain loughs with stony, shelving shore lines. The angler walks or wades along the shore and fishes as he goes. The amount of water that can be covered in this way is limited by how far the angler can cast and how deep he wades. This kind of fishing is usually carried out on remote loughs and can be enormously enjoyable if engaged in by one or two anglers sharing a whole lough. It is not possible on loughs with reedy and soft silty margins. Nor is it much fun to fish a big lough from the shore. The eye tends to wander too often to distant but unreachable productive areas. The shores of the big limestone loughs are frequently covered with bushes and trees and underfoot the margins may be either of reeds and silt and too deep to wade or consist of a wild chaos of boulders and rocky outcrops that make walking and fishing well nigh impossible.

The alternative is to take to a boat and if the lough is big, an outboard motor also becomes a necessity. Clinker built boats have been used for generations by trout anglers on Irish loughs (see page 74). These are boats built specially for the purpose. They vary in length and the width of the beam depending on the size of the lough and the principal requirement of a lough fishing boat is that, when trimmed, it should drift squarely in front of the wind. A good drifting boat should not 'run' to either the bow or the stern. Originally, these boats were built of larch, oak and elm but nowadays, they are mainly constructed of fibre glass. Every angler must

Overleaf
*Fishing the
small rocky
inlets known as
'the Cuts' on
Lough Mask in
County Mayo*

THE BUZZER

'Buzzer' is the common name given by anglers to several species of large chironomid (non-biting midges) that hatch mainly between May and July. They can be grey, olive or ginger in colour and have a habit of flying rapidly along the lough surface. They are widely distributed, occurring mainly on loughs but occasionally on deep river pools (e.g. Kells Blackwater) and when they are hatching, they are among the most important of the natural species that trout feed on. Particularly in May and early June, on both the Midland and Western loughs, trout can be seen feeding on them in sheltered bays where the bottom has silt and weed. The hatches are extensive and, given suitable fishing conditions, early morning and evening buzzer fishing is an unforgettable, exhilarating experience. Fishing pupae and emergers is exciting but seeing a big trout take a dry buzzer, particularly the 'balling' buzzer, is pure magic.

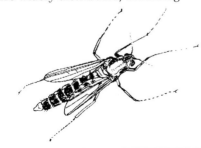

learn the drifting characteristics of his own boat. This determines to which side the stern will point because if the direction of the drift is to be changed, it will be achieved more satisfactorily by manoeuvring a boat towards the stern using the back oar. Building a good lough fishing boat is a great skill. It has to be responsive and easy to row because it is part of the angler's essential equipment. Indeed, it is more. A well-designed boat becomes a reliable, trusted fishing friend, ever obedient to the angler's wish.

THE TROUT'S LARDER

It was the English nymph angler Arthur Cove who said 'The great thing about trout is that they get hungry and when they get hungry, they must eat'. At the start of my lough fishing for trout, another angler advised that 'a rising trout is a dead trout'. I therefore soon learned that to become a competent lough trout fisher, it is necessary to learn about what, when, where and how the trout eats.

The lough trout's diet changes throughout the season as different food items become available. So a basic knowledge of the chief items on the menu is helpful, as is an understanding of the seasons in which they are available, the parts of the lake they occupy and whether they are eaten near the bottom, in mid-water, at or in the surface film or sitting right on top of the water.

It is well known that brown trout are primarily bottom feeders searching out their food among the rocks and vegetation or just above the silt. However, they are nothing if not opportunists and they will also feed at the surface on emerging insects, egg-laying insects or terrestrial insects that get blown on to the water. They will even feed on the fry of coarse fish.

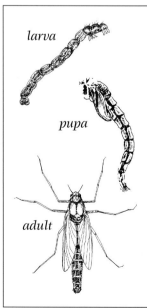

larva

pupa

adult

THE BLOODWORM:
A SHEELIN PHENOMENON

The larvae of chironomids are worm-like creatures and either blood red or pale olive in colour. The red ones are among the few insects to contain haemoglobin in their blood, hence the name, bloodworm. They live in little burrows in the mud at the bottom of loughs. The late J R Harris, author of *An Angler's Entomology*, noted in the late 1940s that they sometimes leave their burrows and swim to the surface. In 1994 Stuart McTeare, who was living at Finea on the shores of Lough Sheelin, made the angling connection when he observed trout feeding on them in late July in near calm conditions. He then proceeded to tie a simple imitation of seal's fur which he fished dry and the trout took it freely. Thanks to Stuart, 'fishing the worm' has now become a recognised technique. The phenomenon occurs in sheltered bays, anytime between early morning and dusk from about 20 July to the end of August.

THE MURROUGH
& THE MIDNIGHT MONSTERS

The murrough or great red sedge (*Phryganea grandis*) is found on limestone rivers and loughs throughout the country. The main hatch occurs in late May and June, often in bog bays and close to small islands and rocky outcrops. The adults emerge in open water and the newly

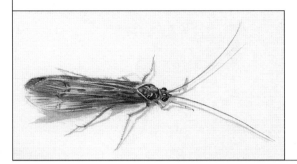

hatched flies scamper along the surface creating a great fuss as they hurry towards the lough shore or river bank. The hatch takes place after dusk and to take full advantage of it, the angler should be positioned facing the afterglow of the sunset to observe the rises.

Murrough fishing can last till 2am and the insect has a reputation for attracting very big trout. Fish feeding on hatching murrough make great swirling rises. Later in the night, when they take the spent flies, the rise is small, just a sip, and your artificial should be cast into the ring of the rise.

Red and black ants occasionally swarm on humid windless days in August and a slight breeze will waft them on to the water. They can cause a widespread rise of trout and a dry artificial imitation will take trout in these circumstances.

Ireland's trout angling season begins about mid-February and ends in early October. In the low water temperatures of winter, the trout's metabolism slows down and it feeds very little – indeed there is little enough to feed on at this time. As winter recedes and the first warmth of spring is felt, the trout start to become active. The first items of food they are likely to encounter are freshwater louse, freshwater shrimps and the occasional corixa, snail, damsel nymph or cased caddis. These are usually found among the rocks in shallow water of three feet or less and wet flyfishing tactics work well.

In the latter part of March and throughout April – the timing will vary from lough to lough – the first major fly hatch occurs. The duck fly is a big chironomid and it normally produces a good rise of trout. The trout mainly take the pupa as it rises to the surface; or in the surface film as it is about to hatch. Duck flies can be found hatching in the morning, afternoon or evening, usually over deep water (15 feet or more), weedy holes and bays.

OVERLEAF
A colourful selection of clinker-style boats at Lough Sheelin, some built in the traditional larch, others in fibre glass

It is essential to have an intimate knowledge of the lough to pin-point the exact location of the hatch. The duck fly hatch is of major importance in the angler's calendar and fishing methods can vary from wet fly to nymph or emerger fishing and occasionally a dry fly is called for. Useful wet fly patterns are Sooty Olive, Fiery Brown, Claret & Mallard , Connemara Black, Peter Ross and Watson's Fancy. Some good chironomid pupae imitations are the Orange Pupa, the Olive Pupa and various emerger patterns. For dry fly, try a William's Favourite or a Grey Duster.

Lake olives begin hatching in mid-April on some lakes and in early May on others. They prefer relatively shallow water with a 'mossy' bottom.

Trout will respond to a wet fly (Greenwell's Glory), an olive parachute pattern or a standard dry fly (Greenwell's Glory or Beacon Beige).

The month of May and early June sees a veritable explosion of fly life of various kinds. Not all lakes have similar hatches.

Some loughs have hatches of claret duns, particularly bog lakes and the bog bays on limestone lakes, such as can be found on Lough Mask. In this situation, a dark claret wet fly is called for on the leader and a dry fly imitation of the dun and spinner may also be required.

The mayfly season begins in early May and lasts into the first or second week of June. Trout begin by feeding on mayfly nymphs. Later they take the emerging fly, the hatched dun and the ovipositing (egg-laying) spinner. Wet Mayfly patterns are legion and they all take fish. The Mosely Mayfly, Adams and Red Humpy are excellent dry flies when trout are taking the duns (or 'green drakes') and the Grey Wulff, Royal Wulff or various Spent Gnat patterns work well when the egg-laying female fly returns to the water.

Some loughs get big hatches of buzzers in May. The buzzer belongs to the same family as the duck fly and can be olive, grey, ginger or even black in colour when it hatches. Depending on the fishing conditions, wet fly tactics, dry fly tactics or nymph tactics may be called for. Various artificial buzzer pupa patterns will take trout as well as the Grey Duster fished dry when trout are taking an adult fly. Sometimes the adults form into clumps on the water and these are known as 'balling buzzers'. It is a phenomenon known only in Ireland. In this situation, a large grey hackled dry fly is called for: something like a large Grey Wulff is perfect. Buzzer hatches may occur at any time from dawn to dusk in the months of May, June and July and anglers must always be on the look out for them. They have a reputation for being a fly of eutropic or enriched loughs but this is not always the case. They can be found hatching on even the most pristine of limestone loughs. All three stages – larva, pupa and adult – of the buzzer's existence is of interest to the trout. The pupae and adult stages have been recognised for years. In recent times, it has been discovered on Lough Sheelin that the larvae, commonly known as 'bloodworm', rise to the surface in late July and August and dry fly imitations, like a red Bob's Bits, have been invented and can give good results (see page 81).

Sedges (caddis flies) come in all sizes from tiny ones just over a quarter of an inch right up to the great big Murroughs and Green Peters, some of which can measure over an inch long. They can be found on loughs as early as March but May to September are the important months. Trout probably recognise sedges by shape and colour tone, rather than by their more subtle characteristics; hence angler's imitations are more suggestive of types rather than species of the natural.

The adult stage is of greatest significance, both just after it emerges and when it returns to the water to lay its eggs and die. The insects are then trapped in the surface of the lough and this explains the effectiveness of the two best known artificial Sedge patterns: the Murrough and the Green

Peter. A particular feature of these patterns is that they can be fished wet or dry. Murroughs hatch at dusk and into the night in late May in bog bays of limestone loughs and they bring up the really big trout. Many smaller sedges (such as the small red sedge, silverhorn sedge, cinnamon sedge, grouse wing sedge and silver sedge) hatch from June to September and trout can be taken on dry fly imitations in quiet bays of big loughs and along the shores of hill loughs.

The caenis (one of the smallest of the upwinged flies) hatches in June and can really get the trout going. A small dry fly imitation works well in sheltered areas by the shore early in the morning.

Shoals of tiny perch and roach fry also appear at the surface in early June and constitute part of the trout's diet for the remainder of the season. The trout will soon discover them and will surround the shoal, lashing the fry with their tails, causing great swirling rises and then quietly cruising about to pick up the dead and injured prey. Trout will often take a small brightly coloured artificial fly (e.g. Peter Ross, Alexandra, Silver Dabbler, or a small floating fry imitation) which is cast into the area of activity and fished static.

Mid-June to mid-July is high summer and usually a quiet time. Any activity that takes place is usually very early in the morning or at dusk and is likely to be brought on by sedges, buzzers or caenis.

A number of things can happen from mid-July to the end of August to get trout moving. Some loughs have a small hatch of mayfly. Chironomids can be active at dawn and dusk. The chironomid larvae, or bloodworms, may ascend to the surface at any time from early morning, during the day or at dusk and bring on a rise of trout. In the last two weeks of July and into early August, there will also be lots of small sedges about and trout take them morning and evening, in fact any time during the day that they come on the water. The big sedge known as the green peter hatches at dusk on the limestone lakes. Terrestrial flies – crane flies (daddies) and grasshoppers – can get blown on to the water particularly in areas where there is rough pasture along the shore and the land has not been fertilised artificially. The daddy can be very important for those who like to dap and an artificial is often fished on a cast of wet flies.

Fishing in September-October is usually confined to working the wet fly – but not entirely. There may be surface activity to lake olives, small sedges, buzzers and perhaps daddies. Trout often feed on daphnia (microscopic water fleas) in September. They are light sensitive and they rise and fall in the water column depending on the intensity of the sunlight. On dull days, they can rise to the surface. The trout follow them up and a small silver fly, like a Silver Invicta, fished on the point can be effective while the other flies on your leader may imitate sedges, olives, buzzers, or just be non-representational, like the Bibio. In recent times, anglers have been adding fluorescent red or green butts or red spots to a variety of traditional

wet flies to attract daphnia-feeding trout. It has proved successful.

The sonaghan trout of Lough Melvin, and possibly Lough Mask, that spend their entire lives in deep water, feed extensively on daphnia. Sonaghan appear to live in shoals which will sometimes rise to the surface as they follow the daphnia in conditions of low light.

It is when they are at or near the surface that they are vulnerable to the angler. At this point they will take insects if they are hatching and can be caught on the usual lough flies although they appear to have a preference for black flies and flies incorporating something red in the dressing. In order to locate the shoals, experienced boatmen will row the boat slowly across the drift while the anglers side-cast, rather than allowing the boat to drift straight downwind.

IDEAL FISHING CONDITIONS

The prevailing weather will dictate not only where we can fish on the lough but also how we fish it: the most appropriate tactics, flylines, flies, etc. Trout dislike extremes of heat or cold, sudden drops in temperature, bright sunshine, squally winds, etc. They like moderate conditions of light, wind and temperature. From the angler's viewpoint, an overcast sky, a steady consistent wind and a mild day are just fine. It means that the trout are not blinded by the sun, the water surface is sufficiently broken to distort their vision, and insects will hatch freely.

ANGLING METHODS FOR THE LOUGH

Wet fly fishing, or lough-style fishing as it is sometimes called, is one of the oldest forms of fishing. Two, three or four flies are cast on the water, allowed to sink and retrieved under the surface. It is carried out in loughs preferably with a good wave and can be done either from the bank or from

Two prime condition brown trout from the lough showing distinct markings. Left: the classic brown trout with red spots and butter yellow flanks. Right: the 'sonaghan' markings with grey-silver flanks, large black spots, black fins and tail.

70

a boat. It is most effective from the boat because it makes the angler more mobile and greater areas of the lough can be covered. In practice, the wet fly fisher searches the water casting the flies in front of a drifting boat and retrieving them back. Usually two anglers fish together, one at the bow, the other at the stern. The boat is always of the clinker built type and should drift low in the water and slowly. Ten to 11¼ foot rods with a floating or intermediate line and three or four flies on the leader is the required tackle. The most productive water is somewhere between three and six feet deep but if natural flies are hatching over deeper water or daphnia have risen to the surface, then this area too can be fished. Short range casting is the order of the day and the flies are retrieved back to the boat just under the surface. It can be a tremendously effective technique.

A heavily dressed fly like a Murrough or a Green Peter is usually fished as an attractor on the top dropper. The art of this method is being able to retrieve the top fly through the waves with the 'eye' of the hook just breaking through the surface. When the flies are cast, they are initially retrieved by hand with two or three short pulls on the line. Retrieving by hand then ceases and the bob fly is controlled from here on by the deft use of the rod tip. When the bob fly can be no longer worked across the waves, it is not cast immediately but held tantalisingly in the surface layer before the next cast is made. This has a huge attraction for trout and they will take it very aggressively. With alternate casts, the flies may be cast in front of the boat and then to the side and drawn across the wave. This has the effect of 'showing' the fly to many more fish. Traditional wet flies work well with this method. When flies are hatching, or terrestrial flies get blown on to the water, the artificial flies used should bear some resemblance in tone and size to the natural insects.

Signs of Rising Trout

If wet fly fishing is used to search the water, rising trout present a whole new situation that may call for a change in tactics from wet flies to dry flies or even emerger patterns as the occasion demands. These tactics are dictated by how the trout are feeding and this can generally be deduced by watching them as they feed. The form the rise takes generally indicates how and on what the trout is feeding. It is a great help therefore to be able to recognise different rise-forms.

The Splashing Rise

A splashing rise occurs when a trout is chasing a fly that it fears is about to lift off from the surface and escape. This is common during hatches of olives, mayflies and sedges, or when they are feeding on fry.

It can be seen a long way ahead. Occasionally a splashing rise may indicate a trout feeding on ascending buzzer pupae. The fish turns sharply at the surface and the splash is caused by the tail breaking the water as it

propels the trout
downward. It is
well to be able to
recognise this rise-form
as these are difficult trout
to attract.

The splashing rise

THE HEAD-AND-TAIL RISE

This is a slow deliberate rise which is usually
indicative of trout taking buzzer pupae hanging in
the surface film. The trout's head appears first
and as he arches his back, the dorsal fin and finally the
tip of the tail is seen. It can also denote a trout taking dead
or dying insects trapped in the surface film. An emerger pattern or a pupa
or nymph will generally get a good response.

The head and tail rise

THE SIP RISE

This denotes a trout lying
very close to the surface,
tilting its head upwards to
sip a spinner or more usually an adult
buzzer trapped in the surface film.
The rise can sometimes even be heard on calm, warm evenings at
dusk. I have witnessed the trout making a snapping sound, as if chomping
their teeth! All that is seen are widening rings that give no clue to the
trout's size. This is a situation that calls for the use of the dry fly.

The sip rise

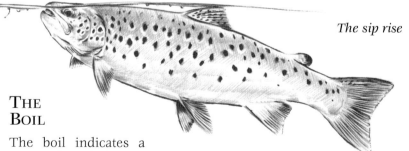

THE BOIL

The boil indicates a
trout that has swum up
towards the surface to intercept an ascending
nymph and then turns down again just before it breaks the
surface. It is frequently observed in a wave when wet fly fishing and if
the rise is covered quickly with an appropriate wet fly (e.g. a Mayfly
pattern at mayfly time) a take will often be the result.

The boil

NYMPH FISHING ON THE LOUGH

When the angler is nymph fishing on loughs he is usually trying to imitate the buzzer or chironomid pupa before it emerges and transforms into its adult state. Now it should be understood that the chironomid family is a big one. The first species to hatch – the duck fly – appears in late March and thereafter, throughout the season, other species occur right into September. The spring and summer hatches are the most prolific and they can happen anytime from early morning to late evening, depending on season and species. Both trout and anglers become very interested when the pupae ascend to the surface. There is usually a lot of surface activity. This often happens in a small ripple or near calm conditions and it is now that the nymph method is used. The ascending pupae often have difficulty in penetrating the surface film. They hang suspended in the film for some considerable time and soon the distinctive slow head-and-tail rise-form of cruising trout taking chironomid pupae can be seen.

In this situation, it is necessary to fish either buzzer pupa patterns, buzzer emerger patterns, Klinkhämer patterns or occasionally even small wet flies (e.g. Sooty Olive, Peter Ross, Blae & Black). They should be cast in front of feeding trout and fished static – do not retrieve them – but an occasional tweak on the line can attract a trout. They are normally fished three on a leader on short droppers and the leader should be thoroughly degreased – or use fluorocarbon monofilament. When trout are feeding like this, close to the surface, their vision is limited. To ensure success, pupa imitations ought to be fished in the top 4–6 inches of water and cast accurately in the path of the trout.

DRY FLY ON THE LOUGH

Dry fly fishing is a technique that has been used on Irish loughs for generations. Indeed, the first trout I ever hooked on a lough was on a dry fly. There is a good reason for this. Irish loughs, especially the limestone ones, have prolific hatches of fly. It normally takes a hatch of fly or a fall of spinners to bring trout to the surface. On a river when trout are feeding on surface flies, the normal procedure is to fish dry. It would appear odd

ABOVE: *A heavily spotted trout from Lough Sheelin*
LEFT: *Waiting for the gnat to fall on the same lake*

indeed, if a trout was observed rising on a still pool in a river, for an angler to cast a team of wet flies to that fish. Indeed, it would probably be regarded as a first class miracle if he hooked it. What is a lough but a huge pool? When trout are taking the duns or spinners of the upwinged flies, adult buzzers, sedges, black gnats, hawthorn, caenis, ants, or even bloodworm, they will normally accept a floating artificial imitation. Irish anglers have come to recognise this and more and more of them are fishing dry, particularly in summer and autumn. Sometimes more than one fly is used and they are usually fished about 4–6 feet apart.

In rivers, trout take up positions and wait for the food to be carried to them on the current. In the lough, trout patrol in search of food and this is particularly true in the case of surface feeders. Because of this patrolling habit, it is necessary for the angler to estimate in advance where the trout will rise next and present the fly in its path. Cruising trout sometimes feed in big circles and sometimes in a straight line. The latter is more likely at mayfly time and the former when they are feeding on sedges or buzzers. When a cruising trout is observed, try to determine its path by observing the pattern of the rises, quietly manoeuvre the boat into position and then present the fly a yard or more in front of the fish.

Any discussion of fishing the artificial fly on a trout lough would not be complete without mentioning the recent development whereby small 'Hoppers' are fished dry in teams of two or three. This technique involves 'fishing the water'. The flies are not usually cast to rising trout but rather are cast on to the water in front of a drifting boat in the hope of inducing a rise. Very successful it can be too, particularly in the July–August period. The flies are treated with floatant and fished on a degreased leader. Favourite shades are fiery brown, claret, red, black, orange, yellow and ginger.

The angler watches the fly and strikes on the take. If the trout is felt but not hooked, it means the strike was probably too late. This advice is worth bearing in mind when any kind of artificial dry fly is being fished on a lough.

In all such circumstances, whether fishing pupae or dry fly from a boat, the angler should remain seated. Unlike bank fishing, there is no background to hide the angler's silhouette and standing up in a boat is a sure way of frightening the trout.

TACKLE FOR THE LOUGH

The type of fishing tackle used is a matter of personal choice and it also depends on the lough. My choice is for three AFTM 6 lines – floating, intermediate and sink-tip, with the option of attaching a fast sinking braided leader. Some use sinking lines including High DS. A through-action 11-foot rod does nicely for wet fly and nymph fishing and a 9½ foot middle to tip action type is fine for the dry fly. The leader is usually of 6lb (3x) monofilament and can measure between ten and eighteen feet depending on the fishing conditions and technique being used. But for really big trout (such as on Lough Sheelin) 8lb or even 10lb is recommended. In other situations, it may be necessary to go down to 4lb (5x). Longer leaders may be required for nymph fishing and when they are used, they must be 'balanced' if they are to turn over, by having a much greater distance between the point fly and the dropper fly than between the dropper fly and bob fly. Other requirements are fly floatant, leader sinking mix, a waterproof cushion and waterproof over-pants and coat that you are sure you can rely on. Finally a life jacket and a small torch completes the list.

DAPPING ON THE WESTERN LOUGHS

Any description of Irish lough fishing would be incomplete without a word about dapping. The method is thought to have originated on Lough Derg but nowadays it is mainly practiced on the great Western loughs, such as Corrib. Visitors to Ireland often marvel at the sight of the long rods – sometimes as many as four – pointing to the heavens from a boat. It is something the whole family can enjoy. They will have lots of fun and there will be much light-hearted banter. It is also a very effective way of fishing for trout and sea trout at certain times and in the right weather conditions.

The first prerequisite is wind, or at least a stiff breeze, which is required to carry the 'blow line' and the fly out over the water. You need a long, light 15 or 16 foot rod. Telescopic models are now available. The line is usually monofilament (15lb BS) held on a standard fly reel, or sometimes a spinning reel. Attached to the monofilament is a 4½ foot length of light dapping floss, wide enough to catch the wind. To this blow line is attached a leader and a bare hook. The leader should not be too long – 7 feet is about right. The hook is a standard size 8 fly hook. The final essential piece of equipment is a custom-made fly box to hold the live insects. It should be waterproof, well ventilated, with a clever, non-return port hole for loading the live insects and a hatch or door for retrieving them.

Dapping does not require a great deal of skill – there is no casting involved – but you will improve with practice. It is a seasonal past-time, dependant on seasonal hatches. It begins in May with the mayfly and continues through June, July, August and into early September. A good practitioner, at the height of the mayfly season, might require up to eight dozen mayflies to last a full day's sport. As the year progresses and mayflies become scarce, murroughs, daddies, grasshoppers and even crickets from the local pet shop can be dapped. In the case of mayflies and daddies, two flies are impaled on the hook together – the others are fished singly. Occasionally, a mayfly and a blue damsel fly are used together and this is considered a good bait for the fresh grilse on Lough Corrib. Artificial bushy dry flies may also be used but they are not considered as effective as the natural flies, except in the case of sea trout in August. The daddy is a much-used sea trout bait. In August and September, two daddies or a grasshopper and a daddy can be impaled together. This is called 'the cocktail'.

The skill in dapping is to keep the fly tripping lightly on the water and so prevent it getting waterlogged. It is more effective if the fly is worked from side to side. When a trout takes the natural dap, the rod must be lowered and you should pause for at least five seconds before the strike is made.

FAVOURITE FLIES FOR THE LOUGH

I doubt if any branch of flyfishing has spawned so many new patterns and variants over the past 25 years as lough fishing. With the explosion of interest in the early 1970s and the increase in the number of anglers tying their own flies thousands of new patterns have emerged. Some have stood the test of time while most will be in fly boxes that are no longer taken fishing. There are certain flies that I always like to carry and the dry flies are as important as the wets. The beauty of fishing in wild places is that you never know what to expect next. This is where the tried and tested patterns come in useful.

ORANGE SHRIMP

Hook: Sizes 12 and 14 Kamasan B160
Tying silk: Brown
Rib: Copper wire
Tail: Orange Antron yarn
Body: Orange Antron dubbing
Hackle: Ginger and blue dun cock palmered sparsely

Early in the season with water temperatures low and food items scarce, trout move into shallow rocky areas in search of food. The above pattern, given to me by Cyril Conlon for fishing in February on the Corrib, is a great fly to attract trout when fished on a sink-tip line and allowed to sink for a few moments. Fish it in short darts.

BIBIO VARIANT

Hook: Sizes 8–12
Tying silk: Black
Rib: Flat pearl tinsel
Body: Seal's fur in three parts; black, hot orange and black
Hackle: Black cock palmered with a brown partridge hackle in front.

The Bibio is a great trout fly in its own right. Murt Folan of Galway came up with this variant which I think is even better for brown trout. He also tied another variant with a body of claret/hot orange/claret seal's fur.

GOLDEN OLIVE BUMBLE

Hook: Sizes 8–12
Tying silk: Brown
Rib: Fine oval gold tinsel
Tail: Golden pheasant topping
Body: Golden Olive Bumble dubbing (Frankie McPhillips' blend)
Body hackles: Golden olive and light red game (ginger) palmered
Shoulder hackle: Blue jay

Kingsmill-Moore has had an enduring influence on Irish lough patterns and the Golden Olive Bumble is one of his best. Here is a fly that has many uses from early season to the autumn. It can be fished on the point early in the season and at lake olive time. It is useful in a sedge hatch in July, but it is at mayfly time that it really excels and a size 10 appears to work best. It is not often that you can make a good fly better. However, Frankie McPhillips seems to have managed just that with his traditional Irish dubbing range. His 'Golden Olive Bumble blend' of dubbing is just the shade that many flytyers and anglers have long been trying to imitate and it has been very successful for many years. It really seems to enhance the original Kingsmill pattern.

SILVER INVICTA

Hook: Sizes 8–12
Tying silk: Black
Rib: Fine oval silver
Tail: Golden pheasant topping
Body: Flat silver tinsel
Hackle: Red game cock palmered

WET AND DRY FLIES FOR THE LOUGH

TOP ROW *Fiery Brown Bits, Claret Smooth Bits, Claret Rough Bits, Bloodworm Bits*
2ND ROW *Buzzer, Red Humpy, Royal Wulff, Small Brown Sedge*
3RD ROW *Golden Olive Bumble, Silver Dabbler, Silver Invicta, Spent Gnat*
BOTTOM ROW *Bibio Variant, Orange Shrimp, Claret Murrough, Mosely Mayfly*

Throat: Blue jay
Wing: Slips of hen pheasant centre tail or hen pheasant secondary wing quill

The Silver Invicta is one of the really great trout flies. It is a good all-rounder for any season and is one of my favourites for the middle dropper. Strongly recommended when trout are feeding on fry.

CLARET MURROUGH

Hook: Sizes 8–10
Tying silk: Black
Rib: Fine oval gold tinsel
Body: Dark claret seal's fur
Hackle: Red-brown cock, palmered
Wing: Dark brown speckled hen
Front hackle: Red-brown cock

Brown sedges are to be found on virtually every lough and the Claret Murrough is a good imitation. When a top dropper fly is required in a big wave, particularly from mid-summer onwards, the Claret Murrough is a personal favourite. It can be fished on the dropper or the point. If trout start to come short, change to the smaller Green Peter.

SILVER DABBLER

Hook: Sizes 8–10 long shank
Tying silk: Black
Rib: Silver wire (to secure palmered hackle)
Tail: Bronze mallard
Body: Claret seal's fur, ribbed with broad, flat silver tinsel and picked out
Hackle: Ginger cock palmered with another, wound at the shoulder
Wing: Bronze mallard tied all around
Head: Black silk built up and varnished

This is a fly to fish on the top dropper in a big wave from mid-summer to the end of the season. Invented by Stuart McTeare, it is one of the Dabbler series – Claret, Golden-Olive and Green being the others – and it will take big trout on the blind, pulling them up from the depths. It is probably at its best when there is a good population of coarse fish fry in the lough. The big head is an important feature as I think this enhances the illusion of a darting fry. It can be fished on a floating line but I prefer it on an intermediate or a sink-tip.

KLINKHÄMER SPECIAL

The Klinkhämer Special's fame has spread from the river (see page 35) to the loughs and I, and many others, have fished it with great success in a range of body colours using Fly-Rite super fine dubbing, flat Mylar tinsel, claret seal's fur and even hare's ear.

RED HUMPY

Hook: Sizes 8–12 Kamasan B170
Tying silk: Red
Tail: Natural tanned elk
Overbody: Elk, as tail
Body: Red tying silk
Wings: Elk, as tail
Hackle: Grizzle and red game cock – use genetic hackles for best results

Looking at this fly, few anglers will credit that an American pattern like this should find a place in an Irish fly box, let alone be listed as one of my top favourite flies. Yet that is exactly how I feel about the Humpy. For several seasons now it has worked wonders at mayfly time both for myself and friends to whom I have given it. It will take trout feeding on freshly hatched green drakes and spinners (gnats or spent gnats) returning to the water. I have even seen trout passing 'better' flies, such as the Mosely Mayfly, to take a Humpy. It is also possible to fish the Humpy 'on the blind' in a ripple or on a big wave – and trout will take it with gusto. Perhaps one of the reasons it is so effective is because it floats so well. This is entirely due to it being dressed with two good quality genetic hackles. Also important is that the proportions of the tail, wings and hackle are correct. I carry a supply in three sizes: 8, 10 and 12. Trout in the Midland lakes (especially Sheelin) will take a size 8 or 10, but on the Western loughs (particularly Conn) a size 10 will take fish, although they sometimes refuse it in favour of a size 12. For anyone who likes to fish dry fly at mayfly time, this is one fly I can heartily recommend. It can also be tied with yellow silk to give a yellow body.

THE BITS

Hook: Sizes 10–14 Kamasan B170
Tying silk: to match body
Body: Claret, fiery brown, red, black or olive seal's fur
Hackle (optional): to match body colour

The Bits series of dry flies first came to my attention in 1996 when Stuart McTeare discovered the effectiveness of a red pattern when bloodworms rose to the surface on Lough Sheelin. They were devised by an English angler named Bob Worts and were originally known as Bob's Bits. Since then, more and more people have taken to fishing a team of two or three Bits in mid-summer and particularly from late July to September when the fishing conditions might otherwise dictate that wet flies are appropriate. After all, it seems logical enough that if we fish the water with a team of wets when there is no hatch and expect to catch a trout, why not offer the trout a non-specific dry fly or better still a number of them. This appears to be the thinking behind fishing Bits 'on the blind'. There is the added attraction that they may represent various small summer terrestrials, blown on to the water. Whatever the attraction may be, trout take them and I personally think it is always more exciting to watch a trout take a dry fly and then hook it successfully. Bits can be tied in two different ways – depending on the prevailing conditions. If fishing in a good wave, I prefer them with the seal's fur well picked out. This aids flotation. In a small ripple on calm conditions, a much slimmer and smaller version is required.

Bits should always be tied with natural seal's fur (rather than a synthetic substitute) as the seal's fur absorbs and retains the floatant better. I rarely use ribbing material, but if it is thought necessary, only fine wire should be applied as even oval tinsel may cause the fly to sink. Fish the Bits by casting them in front of the boat and only retrieve the slack line. A quick false cast is enough to dry the flies. Before lift off, in a big wave, I will sometimes dibble the bob fly and this has frequently induced a take. My favourite colours for Bits are claret, fiery brown – and red for the bloodworm.

SMALL BROWN SEDGE

Hook: Sizes 12–14 Kamasan B170 or B160
Tying silk: Brown
Body: Fly Rite brown dubbing (BCS 87/98)
Wing: Red squirrel tail
Hackle: Red brown or red cock

Anyone who ignores the importance of small sedges on a lough does so at their peril. At least that is my belief. We all know how effective the artificial imitations of murroughs and green peters can be. Small sedges are infinitely more numerous and deserve more attention. I have found the CDC & Elk patterns (see page 35) quite good and have taken some big trout on them as well as a lot of small ones on mountain lakes, but my vote has to go to Michael Kelly's Small Brown Sedge. Fished in calm or low ripple conditions, it has a remarkable propensity for attracting trout and the size 14 version is best. Another point in its favour is the ease with which it can be kept under observation, even at a distance.

THE BUZZER

Hook: Sizes 12–14 Kamasan B160 or B170
Rib: Clear polypropylene
Body: Musk rat fur or rabbit
Hackle: Silver badger

From May onwards, buzzers (midges) begin hatching and returning to the water to lay their eggs. Occasionally during the day, but mostly in the evenings, trout will home in on the adult flies, often making a sipping sound as they take them. In this situation, they are unlikely to take a pupa imitation or an emerger pattern – only the dry fly. The above is a good all-round pattern but it may be necessary to vary the shade of the dubbing to match the colour of the natural. The above dressing (in small sizes) will also take trout feeding on caenis early in the morning.

ROYAL WULFF, MOSELY MAYFLY, SPENT GNAT

These are standard dressings which can be found in *Trout & Salmon Flies of Ireland* (see Bibliography on page 192)

4

THE TROUT'S FOOD

W e fish with concoctions of feathers and fur, silk and tinsel and we call them artificial flies. For centuries, fishermen have been observing the behaviour and feeding habits of trout. It is obvious that the greater part of the trout's diet consists of the various insects they encounter in and on the water. Some are flies with wings but there are other creatures too, like beetles, caterpillars, ants and snails. Trout are great opportunists and they may feed on a whole range of insects, depending on the kind of river or lough they live in, the time of season and sometimes even the time of the day.

Anglers are also aware that trout will sometimes be quite selective and choose only one particular insect, ignoring all the others. In this situation if the fisherman carefully observes the insect that the trout is feeding on, and by using an artificial fly that is roughly similar to it in size, shape and colour, the chances of success increase. It doesn't always work but, generally, anglers who can select the right fly and fish it in the right place and in the right way, are more successful. It may be simply a matter of having confidence in a fly – self confidence is a wonderful ally. People who are confident are more alert and perform better in all sorts of ways.

LEFT: The Midland loughs of Sheelin, Ennell and to a lesser extent Derravaragh are noted for their 'Spent Gnat' fishing. Sometimes the fall of spent gnat can be quite astonishing. Here, they have taken a rest on the broad back of Sheelin boatman, Denis O'Keeffe.

OBSERVATION AND FLY SELECTION

In the introduction, we listed observation, river craft, casting and fly selection as major factors in successful flyfishing. Here we are dealing with two of them – observation and fly selection. There is no doubt that one becomes a better angler by learning about the more important insects on which trout feed. This knowledge includes being able to recognise various insects or families of insects, and knowing a little about the life cycle and general behaviour of the more important species.

In other words, a little knowledge makes choosing a fly from your flybox easier. The study of insects is called entomology. University students spend long years studying insects and some become lecturers and even Professors of Entomology. Many of them are not anglers and never will be. Entomologists identify species of fly by reference to precise details and the structure of parts which are often microscopic in size.

But you don't have to become a Professor in order to be a good angler!

It is perfectly adequate for an angler to be able to identify flies by their superficial characteristics such as shape, size and colour. We look at the shape of their wings, how many they have, how they hold them, whether an insect has a tail or not, etc. We use our eyes to spot different physical characteristics and in that way it is possible to consign most of the insects in Ireland that interest trout into four main groups:

1 Upwinged flies (olives and mayflies)
2 Roof-shaped winged flies (sedges or caddis flies)
3 Flat-winged flies (midges, buzzers, gnats, etc)
4 The rest (a variety of both aquatic and terrestrial insects)

All of them are found in greater or lesser numbers on both rivers and loughs.

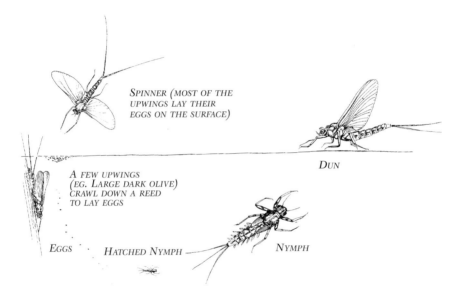

SPINNER (MOST OF THE UPWINGS LAY THEIR EGGS ON THE SURFACE)

DUN

A FEW UPWINGS (EG. LARGE DARK OLIVE) CRAWL DOWN A REED TO LAY EGGS

EGGS   *HATCHED NYMPH*   *NYMPH*

LIFE CYCLE OF AN UPWINGED FLY

1. UPWINGED FLIES (OLIVES AND MAYFLIES)

The Latin name of this family is Ephemeroptera.

When I first took an interest in the flies trout feed on, the many different names that anglers gave to this group of flies caused more confusion than anything else. Suffice it to say that anyone referring to a mayfly, an olive, a sub imago, an imago, a dun, a spinner, a spent gnat or a gnat has an upwing fly in mind. The group contains species as diverse as the mayfly, the blue-winged olive and the caenis. The principal characteristics by which we recognise an upwing fly are its sail-like wings and its long tails - all upwinged flies have either two or three tails.

The Nymph

The first stage of its life of interest to the trout is the nymph. It lives on the bottom among the stones, in the vegetation or even burrowed into the silt at the bottom of a river or lough for between six months and two years, depending on the species. Trout will have them if they can find them. Naturally those that live among the stones and vegetation are more readily available.

When they are ready to leave the water and hatch, they become active and restless. They even make test runs to the surface and at this stage the trout get very interested and begin feeding on them as they return to the bottom. On the final ascent, the majority of them become so buoyant from a bubble of gas that has collected in their wing buds that they get carried to the surface and are unable to return. They remain trapped in the surface film until the wing case splits open and out climbs a winged fly. It is then called a dun – or sub imago to the scientist (or 'green drake' in the case of mayflies, while the smaller species are often referred to as 'olives' or 'olive duns').

The Dun (sub imago)

The dun must remain on the surface of the water until its wings are dry enough for it to fly to the bank or to the underside of a leaf or a blade of grass. On a dry, warm day this happens quickly. On a humid, damp day on the river, it gets carried downstream by the current. On a lough it can remain stuck to the surface or be blown along by the wind and carried by the waves all the way to the shore where it will climb out on the stones. Life becomes very dangerous for duns on wet, murky days. A lot of them get hopelessly drowned and become easy pickings for trout.

As the name 'dun' suggests, the fly looks a dull matt colour at this stage of its life.

The Spinner (imago)

The dun stage can last for as little as a few minutes (in the case of caenis) to several days (in the case of mayflies) before it transforms again by shedding its skin to become a spinner or imago. This stage of the mayfly is called the 'gnat' by anglers. In the case of the other smaller species it is referred to as a spinner. It is after transformation to the spinner stage that mating takes place.

The females then return to the water to lay their eggs and begin the cycle all over again. Different species have different ways of doing this. Some, like the mayfly, land on the water. Others, like the blue-winged olive, fly along close to the surface and let the water wash the eggs from their tail ends. A few, like the large dark olive, climb down a reed, post or rock and lay the eggs on the bottom.

After the egg laying, the spinners are spent and die almost immediately. These are known as 'spent gnats'. During the egg laying and when they have died, they are very visible and vulnerable to the trout, particu-

Overleaf
If your trout is for the pot it is always worth using the marrow spoon to see what it has been eating. In this case it revealed a diet of caddis and snails

FESTIVAL OF THE MAYFLY

This is the largest of Ireland's upwinged flies on both river and lough. The hatch begins about 10 May on the river Boyne and on the shallow, warmer loughs such as Carra, and elsewhere it is about 7 to 10 days later.

An especially warm or cold winter and spring can advance or retard the mayfly's appearance by a week. The arrival of the mayfly (*Ephemera*

danica) heralds the true beginning of summer when the hawthorn is in bloom and air temperatures are rising. It creates a carnival atmosphere, particularly around the famous mayfly loughs, where accommodation, boat and gillie availability, are all at a premium. Whole families often take to the boat and go 'dapping', probably the most popular mayfly fishing method on the Western loughs.

Trout feed eagerly on the emerging nymphs, duns (green drakes) and later, the spinners (spent gnats). Fishing artificial flies gives good results – wet fly or dry fly depending on the circumstances. For many, spent gnat dry fly fishing is the cream and generally produces above-average sized trout.

larly in the latter stage as they lie spread-eagled on the water.

UPWINGS FROM THE TROUT'S PERSPECTIVE

Upwinged flies, at all three stages of their existence (nymph, dun and spinner), form an important part of the trout's diet, on both rivers and loughs. An artificial nymph imitation is much more widely used on rivers than on loughs, with the exception of the mayfly nymph which, at a certain time of the year, is a significant source of food in both moving and still waters. Imitations of the smaller duns and spinners are probably of greater importance to the river angler although, again, the larger mayfly duns and spinners (spent gnats) are of prime importance on the loughs as well.

UPWINGED FLIES OF THE RIVER

While there are several dozen species of upwinged flies on both rivers and lakes, I believe it is only really necessary for the angler to be familiar with the more important ones. This amounts to about a dozen and if we know a little about the season in which they occur and the time of day that they hatch we are well on our way to understanding them and their role in the trout's diet. Bear in mind that neither the flies nor the trout are obliging enough to conform to strict timetables. Flies may appear at times other than those listed. Trout too can be perfidious, ignoring the most prolific hatches. The table on page 49 sets out some of the more important upwinged river flies and suggests some matching artificials.

UPWINGED FLIES ON THE LOUGH

The range of upwinged flies on Irish loughs is limited and less confusing than on rivers.

The lake olive is the first to make an appearance about mid-April and the hatch continues into May. The fly occurs again in a smaller size and paler shade in September. It is mainly an insect of the limestone loughs and hatches over the shallower water with a 'mossy' weed-covered bottom. Hatches can be sporadic and prolific in both the morning and afternoon. Trout are mainly interested in the hatching flies and occasionally take the duns as they sit on the water, drying their wings. Wet fly fishing is the traditional method at lake olive time and a small Greenwell's Glory, Sooty Olive or a Hare's Ear, are the flies to use. Trout may also take a dry fly such as a Greenwell's Glory, a Parachute Olive or one of the emerger patterns.

The mayfly hatch typically begins in early May though this can vary according to the season and the lough. The nymphs are large and so also is the dun or green drake and the spinner or gnat.

Local knowledge is usually necessary on the big loughs to know where the best hatches occur. The nymphs become active for some weeks before the hatch occurs and trout notice and begin feeding on them. If the weather is dry and hot when the flies are hatching, the trout continue to take the nymph because the duns fly off too quickly. In periods of high humidity or wet weather the dun, or green drake, remains on the water for some time and provides good dry fly fishing. If there is a strong wind and a big wave on the lough, a lot of the duns get drowned and wet fly fishing gives best results.

The duns fly to the shore where they take refuge in a leafy bush and remain there for some days. They transform to spinners during this time and, some days later, when the weather is mild they will mate and the females fly out on the water to lay their eggs. This normally happens after 7pm but as the season progresses, it can happen anytime in the afternoon or evening depending on weather conditions and air temperature. A fall of spent gnat is manna from heaven for the trout and they cruise rapidly and take the egg-laying dead and dying flies in a fairly predictable pattern of rises till dusk. At dusk and more especially in the early morning the male spinners fall on the water close to the shore. This can also cause a few trout to feed close to the shore.

Wind lanes on a lough are an important feature at mayfly time and ought not to be ignored. The spent flies in particular seem to congregate in them and so too do the trout, even during the day. They are one of the first features I look for at mayfly time.

The claret dun is an important fly on mountain loughs and is sometimes important in 'bog bays' of limestone loughs, such as Carra. It has a very dark almost black body and three tails. It hatches from early May to the middle of July. The hatching dun is of most interest to the trout and the angler. For wet flyfishing use a small dark Claret & Mallard and for dry fly a big Iron Blue Dun pattern will suffice.

Dappers find their store of flies on trunks and under the leaves on the sheltered side of trees and bushes. At times like this they can easily be collected and stored in a box.

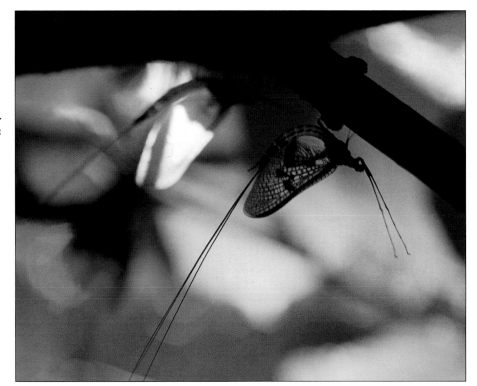

The caenis or 'fisherman's curse' hatches in June and July in the early morning (7am) and again in the evening. Trout feed on the nymphs in the surface film and on the duns and spinners in the calm areas close to the shore. The early morning trout are easier to fool and I have had good success with a size 16 Grey Duster fished on a fine leader in calm water close to the shore.

2. ROOF-WINGED FLIES (SEDGE OR CADDIS FLIES)

These flies all belong to the order *Tricoptera*. They are recognisable by the manner in which they fold their wings over their bodies in the shape of a roof. Anglers in Ireland usually call them sedges or Peters. They vary in size from tiny specimens a quarter of an inch long, to great big ones of well over an inch.

Trout love sedges. There are hundreds of different species but the great thing about them is that they all have the same basic silhouette and shape. Trout normally see the adults from below, in silhouette, and once the size and shape of the artificial is right, the colour, or how the artificial is dressed, does not seem to matter very much. Sedges are widespread on both rivers and loughs. They hatch in every month of the angling season from March to October with July and August the peak months. I sometimes think they are more important than the upwinged flies, with the exception of the mayfly.

FAMILY OR FAKE?
A sedge poses
on the lid of a
box of artificial
imitations

LIFE CYCLE OF THE SEDGE

The life cycle of the sedge is in four stages: egg, larva, pupa and adult. The majority of immature larvae build a little house for themselves of sticks, sand, pieces of vegetation, snail shells etc. At this stage in its life it is often referred to as the 'cased caddis' or 'stick fly' because of its appearance. The larger ones can look just like a piece of a broken stick, about one and a half inches long. The case acts as a camouflage but it does not prevent trout eating them, especially in spring, and an artificial Stick Fly, fished near the bottom of a river can be deadly.

When the time comes, the larva changes into a pupa (see below). When fully formed the pupa ascends to the surface and very quickly

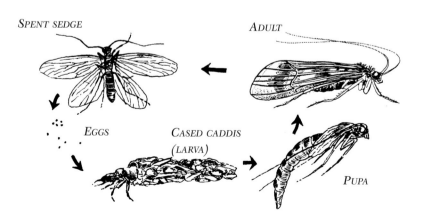

SPENT SEDGE

ADULT

EGGS

CASED CADDIS
(LARVA)

PUPA

LIFE CYCLE OF
THE SEDGE OR
CADDIS

hatches out into an adult on the surface, in open water. These are the important ones for trout and fishermen. As soon as it hatches, the sedge creates quite a disturbance by skittering across the surface of the water or trying to swim against the river in full view of the trout. Eventually their wings dry and they fly off. Some of them scurry all the way to the shore. They can live under a stone or old log for up to a month before mating and returning to lay their eggs.

Trout love to eat sedges. They are large, tasty morsels and highly conspicuous as they scurry across the surface.

Trout will also feed on sedges as they float dead in the upper surface layers of water after laying their eggs. This probably explains the effectiveness of fishing artificial sedge patterns like the Green Peter and Murrough as wet flies.

In my experience of sedge fishing, a relatively small number of artificial patterns in a range of sizes is all that is required. The same flies can be fished on either river or lough to equally good effect. You should use a pattern that offers a good silhouette of the natural. Some sedges are in a constant whirl on the water. Hackled flies are best for imitating these active insects. They look as though they are in motion, even when they are sitting still! On other occasions, such as late in the evening, a streamlined pattern with little or no hackle is a better option.

RIVER SEDGES

The first sedge to appear in significant numbers on the limestone rivers in mid-May to mid-June is the grey flag. A small pale sedge, it hatches during the day in big numbers, flutters on the surface and is taken with gusto by the trout.

The black caperer, or welshman's button, is a larger and darker sedge of the southern rivers. It hatches by day and in the evening from mid-May to the end of July and occasionally in August. It is always taken by trout most eagerly.

The murrough is one of Ireland's biggest sedges: dark brown and well over an inch long. It hatches on limestone rivers, on deep pools at dusk and it flutters temptingly on the water. It attracts the big trout.

Some green peters are as big as the murrough. They have mottled wings and hatch in much the same locations as the murrough. The green peter's time is late July and August.

Finally, there is a whole range of small and medium sized sedges that hatch mostly in the evening in open water during the summer. Most sedges will bring on a rise of trout if there are enough of them on the water.

LOUGH SEDGES

The first small sedges begin hatching in March on both limestone and neutral loughs and trout will take them.

The murrough is the first significant sedge to hatch in big numbers. It appears at dusk in late May to early June, in 'bog bays' and flutters on the surface. Black sedges and silverhorns hatch at this time as well.

Throughout the summer a range of sedges can be seen on the loughs, particularly in the evening. The Welshman's Button occurs on Lough Ennell during the day and evening in May/June. One of the most important is the green peter of the Midland loughs in late July and early August. Also present are silverhorns, cinnamon sedges and various small sedges, some with grey wings and green-olive bodies and others with brown wings and black bodies.

ABOVE
When the blood-worm is to be seen near the surface it will surely be on the trout's menu and you would be wise to try a red Bits pattern, well greased.

3. FLAT-WINGED FLIES (BUZZERS, BLACK GNATS, DADDIES)

The 'true' flat-winged flies belong to the order *Diptera* and there are literally thousands of species. Even non-anglers are familiar with some of them, e.g. daddy-long-legs, house flies, biting midges and mosquitoes to name but a few. If you look at any of them, they have the same characteristics, namely, six legs, and two flat short wings that extend only two thirds of the way along a well segmented body. Now most of those mentioned above are land insects and some of them are important in their own right to anglers.

ABOVE
A good picture of the 'gillaroo' trout showing its bulging belly. It feeds predominantly on snails and has developed an enlarged, muscular stomach for dealing with shells.

However, there is an aquatic branch of the *Diptera* order as well, with close on four hundred members. Lough anglers call them by various names, the most common of which are buzzers, duck flies or chironomids. On the rivers they are usually referred to as midges.

Let's look at the flies we call buzzers or chironomids first and deal with the terrestrials separately. What we have here is a family of flies made up of many different species. The large dark chironomids that hatch in March and April are usually called duck flies. It is important to note that 'duck fly' is a generic name which covers several different species. Anglers call any flat-winged fly that hatches in a lough from May to September, simply a buzzer or a chironomid.

LIFE CYCLE OF THE BUZZER

The life cycle of the buzzer is egg, larva, pupa and adult. The larva is either olive, brown or crimson in colour. The pupa can vary in colour from claret, to red, olive, grey, or black. At the point of hatching, a pupa can even change colour, say from orange to black, as it oxidises in the air. Similarly, the adults can be different colours. Some have black bodies, others ginger, olive, grey etc. For the angler, observation of the colour and understanding

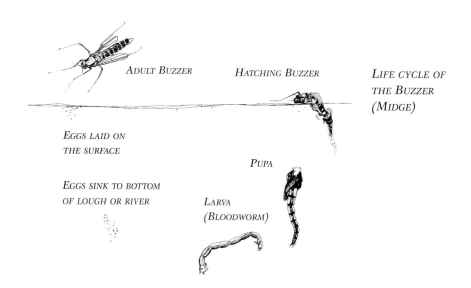

ADULT BUZZER   HATCHING BUZZER   LIFE CYCLE OF
                                   THE BUZZER
                                   (MIDGE)

EGGS LAID ON
THE SURFACE

                        PUPA

EGGS SINK TO BOTTOM
OF LOUGH OR RIVER   LARVA
                     (BLOODWORM)

the stage of its life in which the insect is being taken by the trout, can be vitally important. Trout seem sometimes to home in on particular colours of buzzers and at such times it is important to fish the correct tone or colour. This is not something that can be learned from a book but rather by observation on the lough and exchanging experiences with other knowledgeable anglers.

The buzzer larvae are worm-like creatures, up to an inch long. Some burrow into the mud on the bed, some live among the lough bottom vegetation and some live in little tubes of silt stuck to stones. At this stage they are of no great interest to the trout or the angler except in one exceptional circumstance. In 1995 it was noted for the first time in an Irish lough, that red and crimson buzzer larvae rose to the surface on Lough Sheelin in July and August. Some actually lay flat on the surface. The trout then fed on them voraciously, as if taking adult flies, and dry fly tactics with Bloodworm imitation flies gave good results. The phenomenon has been repeated in every subsequent year. I have not heard of it occurring elsewhere in Ireland.

Chironomids can hatch at any time of the season but the predominant hatches occur in the months March to the end of July. The early season hatches occur during the day, often in very cold weather. Later, the hatches extend into the evening and summer hatches occur mainly in the early morning and the evening. The best fishing conditions are with a light breeze and a ripple on the water.

Chironomid pupae have difficulty escaping through the surface. They hang vertically or lie horizontally in the top layer for some time before hatching and are very vulnerable to trout. Chironomids, depending on the season, usually favour certain areas of loughs that both the trout and the anglers soon get to know about.

The adult flies often sit on the water for some time prior to taking off to the shore. They are vulnerable to trout at this time and again when the females return to lay their eggs. Buzzers are usually in a constant whirl on the water when they return to lay their eggs. They are best imitated by hackled flies like the Grey Duster which look as though they are in motion, even when conditions are relatively calm.

A unique feature of some species of buzzer is that in warm weather in May and June, as many as two dozen males will attempt to mate with one female on the water. They form a large clump nearly as big as a golf ball that rolls along on the surface of the lough usually in sheltered bays. The phenomenon which, as far as I know, only occurs on Irish loughs, is known to anglers as the 'balling buzzer' and the trout are quick to notice it. To give you some idea of the size of the clump, the artificial imitation should be dressed Palmer-style on a size 8 long shank hook.

4. SOME EXTRA TERRESTRIALS (AND OTHERS)

While most anglers will be familiar with the principal aquatic insects, it is wise to be aware of other creatures like the crustaceans, corixa, and the many terrestrial insects that may occasionally land on rivers and loughs. They will all form part of the trout's larder.

Alder

You would be forgiven for mistaking the alder (*Megaloptera*) for a sedge. It has black-brown wings, and black head, body and legs. It is normally found around lakes in May and June – but in small numbers – and the trout take little heed of it. It has a strange life cycle. The eggs are laid on the land. They hatch into larvae which then crawl into the water. When ready to hatch, the larvae crawl ashore again.

Black Gnat

The black gnat (*Bibio johannis*) is a terrestrial which appears on the river in swarms in warm, calm weather from late April to September. There are several species and they are all small. The wings are flat and shiny and the body is dark brown to black. They often swarm on the sheltered side of a bush or tree. Their life span is very short and individual insects continually fall or get blown on to the water. The black gnat is hugely important on rivers and also on reed-fringed, sheltered bays of the Midland loughs.

Corixa

The corixa (*Herniptera*), or lesser waterboatman, looks like a small beetle. It lives in shallow water and must swim regularly to the surface to replenish its air supply. At the surface, it grabs a bubble of air and swims to the bottom again. I have seen it in trout stomachs as early as April but it appears to be a more important part of the trout's diet in September.

Daddy-long-legs

Everyone is familiar with the daddy, or crane fly. Late July and August is when it is most plentiful. A terrestrial insect of the *Diptera* order, it gets blown on to the water, particularly loughs. Trout take them, as do sea trout and I have seen autumn grilse rise to them on the river. The natural fly can be dapped (usually two flies placed side-by-side) and the artificial imitation seems more effective if fished wet on the loughs. A floating pattern can also be useful.

Damselflies

Damselflies (*Odonata*) are aquatic and appear around loughs and rivers in June–July. Trout feed on the nymphs, particularly early in the season when food is scarce. Very occasionally, damselflies fall on the water and are taken by trout. Anglers often dap two damselflies on Lough Corrib for grilse.

Flying ants

Ants (*Hymenoptera*) are terrestrials but in late July/early August on windless, humid days the winged ants will swarm. The lightest breeze can land them all on the river or lake and this inevitably brings on a frenzied rise of both brown trout and sea trout. The ants I have seen have always been either red or brown.

Freshwater louse

The freshwater louse (*Crustacea*) feeds on decaying vegetation on the bottom of loughs. It appears to be most plentiful in late winter and early Spring and is often found in trout's stomachs.

Freshwater shrimp

Freshwater shrimps (*Crustacea*) are found in both rivers and loughs. They inhabit the shallower stony and weedy areas and trout feed on them regularly. They are very important early in the season (March).

Grasshopper

Grasshoppers (*Orthoptera*) can be found in old pastures (often near rocky outcrops) that are unaffected by artificial fertilisers or agricultural pesticides. A single grasshopper, impaled on the hook, makes an excellent dapping bait for brown trout – also sea trout – especially in the month of

MARROW SCOOP FINDINGS
Above: The bloodworm and corixa have been eaten with relish by this Sheelin trout. Right: Sedge pupa with distinctive yellow and brown markings

August. The colour of the natural fly varies from bright olive to claret and the tops of the legs on some are bright orange.

Hawthorn Fly

The hawthorn (*Bibio marci*) appears on the land for about three weeks in late April and May at the same time as the bush of the same name is in bloom. It looks like a housefly but is distinguished by long black dangling legs. A weak flier, it gets blown on to the water and trout absolutely love it. Fish a dry fly on the river and the same fly can be fished wet on the lough.

Heather fly

The heather fly, *Bibio pomonae*, forms an important part of both brown and sea trout's diet from July to September on loughs surrounded by heather. The late Major Charles Roberts of Burrishoole gave us the perfect artificial: the Bibio.

House fly

The house fly and the blue-bottle (*Diptera* order) occasionally reach the water during the summer, particularly deep river pools with overhanging branches. They are always of interest to the trout, especially the bigger trout. A black-bodied Klinkhämer (hackled with blue dun) will get a response, or else simply try a large Black Gnat.

Reed smuts

Reed smuts are very small and are often wrongly called 'black gnats'. The reed smut (*Simulium* spp.) is aquatic and the pupa comes up in a bubble of air in May and June. They are mostly found on rivers where they will bring on a big rise of trout. They are also found along sheltered reedy shores on limestone lakes and trout will take the adults in the calm water close to the edge.

Snails

Several species of snail (*Crustacea*) live in loughs and rivers. They form a very important part of the trout's diet, and gillaroo trout, in particular, feed extensively on them. They are of interest to the angler on loughs that don't have gillaroo when they come to the surface in July, August and September. If trout are observed heading and tailing at this time, and there are no apparent insects about on the water, then look out for snails in the surface film.

Soldier beetle

The soldier beetle (*Cantharis rustica*) has a distinct orange head and wings. It can be observed from April to August flitting around in the rough lakeside vegetation and on the islands in the big loughs. On calm days, it may also be spotted on the water. Brown trout have a particular liking for it and a Fiery Brown Bits, fished dry, is a great artificial imitation.

Moths

Most moths are nocturnal. Some end up in the river in June and July. They flutter and try to become airborne again, thereby drawing the attention of the trout. A well-hackled imitation like the White moth (O'Reilly) can often interest a late trout.

5

SEA TROUT FISHING

I have never met an all-round game angler for whom fishing for sea trout does not strike a special chord. These shy, dashing creatures can snatch a fly at lightning speed and pound-for-pound they will make the reel sing and the line slice the water as well as any fish that takes the fly.

Sea trout are basically brown trout that migrate to sea at an early age, just as salmon do. The purpose of the sea journey seems to be to find richer feeding grounds where they can grow to maturity before returning to the freshwater to spawn and begin the cycle all over again. Brown trout and sea trout share a common ancestor. A brown trout is a sea trout that did not go to sea. On the other hand, small brown trout, particularly in small rivers and loughs all around the coast are all potential sea trout.

Once upon a time, it was fashionable for anglers to kill all the small 'brown' trout that they caught when fishing for sea trout. This has now been confirmed to be a dreadful mistake as scientists have learned that potential sea trout may live in the freshwater for several years before becoming smolts. About half of them go to sea at two years of age but some can remain in the river for five or even six years.

This chapter is not intended as a scientific treatise on sea trout. We are only interested in their behaviour and life style in so far as it relates to angling.

DISTRIBUTION

Sea trout, known in many parts of Ireland as 'white trout', are found in varying numbers in the estuaries of most rivers around the coast. They are most plentiful in the smaller river systems and indeed are often the only kind of trout worth fishing for in the small acid river and lough systems all along the north, west and south west coast.

River systems with a series of loughs running back from the coast into the hinterland are especially suited to producing prolific sea trout runs. Big numbers of sea trout may also be found in the lower reaches of the larger limestone rivers. Evidence from rivers like the Boyne and Corrib show that they don't seem to migrate far upstream.

SIZE RANGE

Small sea trout are called by different names – finnock, juners or harvesters – depending on the season and the part of the country. Finnock is probably the most common name in Ireland. This group consists of fish that have migrated in spring and spend between two and five months feeding in the estuary and close to the coast before returning to the freshwater in big numbers. They average between eight and ten ounces and can be encountered by anglers from July to the end of the fishing season. They make up the greater part of any sea trout population.

Medium-sized sea trout – fish in the 1½ –3 lb range – are of greatest interest to the anglers. They have spent either one or two winters feeding at sea. They are big healthy trout, returning to spawn for the first time and if hooked when fresh in the river or lough, they will jump up to eight times and fight like demons.

Finally, there are the big sea trout ranging in size from 4–10lb. They are not plentiful but they are the specimen fish that every sea trout angler dreams of catching at least once in his life. These trout are multi-spawners. After spawning in November, they return to the sea as soon as possible, feed for three or four months and return in prime condition to the fresh water. They normally return in April and those of them that are caught are usually taken in April or early May. Once in the freshwater for a few weeks, they lie low by day and are virtually impossible to catch. Like salmon, sea trout are caught at the times they are active. Small and medium-sized sea trout may be active during the day but the big ones, once in freshwater for any length of time are only active at night or on a dropping flood. The average size of a rod-caught Irish sea trout is probably about 1½ lb. The large number of small finnock keeps this average down. It is the two and a half or three pounder that makes the day memorable. In many parts of Ireland, sea trout are known as 'white trout.'

FEEDING HABITS OF THE SEA TROUT

Overleaf
A fine sea trout, fresh from the tide and showing a characteristic livery: silver flanks, white belly and small black spots – all of which develop during its time in saltwater.

Sea trout, unlike salmon, feed in fresh water – but not much. They certainly do not do so with the same voracity as brown trout, their stomachs are never bulging full. Frequently, you will find the stomach is empty and if it contains food it will only be a few items like beetles, midges or land insects. There is one very good reason for this. Food is normally scare in fast, impoverished sea trout waters. That is why they went to sea in the first place. However if food gets blown onto the water they will have a go. It is never enough and does not happen often. This is why sea trout lose their condition in fresh water. A plump three pounder in early July can weigh less than 2½ lb in September.

So, unlike the brown trout which the angler attempts to lure with something that represents the food it is accustomed to, the sea trout requires a different approach.

THROUGH THE EYES OF THE SEA TROUT

The stimulus for the sea trout taking a fly is triggered by sight. It would appear that its sight and particularly its night sight is very good. How else can it pick out and take a lightly dressed size 10 fly fished deep in pitch darkness. This acuity of vision has other consequences too, especially for the angler. Our sea trout is quick to notice anything untoward that intrudes on its environment. It has been to sea and has been at the mercy of numerous predators, from sea fish to seals and cormorants, any of which would be happy to make a meal of it. For this reason, it is constantly on guard, ready to scurry off in a flash at the slightest sign or sound of trouble. This is something we should be aware of and avoid clumsy, noisy walking on river banks, standing up in boats, the splashing of oars, the revving of an outboard motor or any disturbance of a piece of water about to be fished.

FLY PRESENTATION

The importance of good casting and delicate fly presentation cannot be emphasised enough where sea trout are concerned. I have mentioned above how timid they can be. The flies must arrive on the water quietly and without fuss. Any sign of sloppy casting or noisy presentation and the angler will be wondering if there are any sea trout in the water at all.

LOUGH, RIVER AND ESTUARY

Nearly every coastal river system in Ireland holds sea trout. The majority of good sea trout systems have one or two, or even a chain of loughs, each of which has its own characteristics. My own experience of sea trout has been mainly on the west coast fisheries from Donegal to Kerry. Hence, I can only write about my experience there and assume that sea trout elsewhere behave in much the same way. For ease of understanding it is best to deal with lough and river fishing separately.

SEA TROUT LOUGHS

Sea trout loughs are mainly acid waters located along the west and south-west coast. They range in size from little more than big pools on rivers, like Derreen Lough at Fermoyle, to large glacial waters up to three miles long like Glenveagh Lough in Donegal.

SEA TROUT SEASONS

Depending on the location, the first run of sea trout begins in March and April. These early fish are the big multi-sea winter fish and the numbers of them are not large. Little or no sea trout fishing is done in March and April and, apart from occasional fish that are caught by anglers while trolling and flyfishing for salmon, the sea trout quickly go stale and become difficult to

Night-time fishing for sea trout on the lough should begin at about 10.30pm. It is best if there is no moon.

catch. The big fish appear to be especially plentiful in Co. Kerry, but no doubt other areas get them too.

The main run of sea trout proper – fish in the 1–2lb range – begins in June. It reaches its peak in the south-west about the third week of June and a month later in Connemara, Mayo and Donegal. In August, September and early October, the runs consist mainly of finnock. Among them will be some bigger sea trout.

The whole purpose of the sea trout entering fresh water is to spawn. Hence at every opportunity presented by a rise in water, their instinct is to forge further upstream through the river pools and from one lough to the next till eventually in November they have reached the spawning streams in the head waters.

As I mentioned earlier, sea trout only feed a little in fresh water. Fresh run trout are always catchable, but when they are in a river or lough for a long time without a rise in water, they become difficult to catch. They rest, they probably sleep to conserve energy, they go stale and lose their silver colour. It takes a change in the weather conditions or a rise of water level to wake them up and make them active and catchable again.

Sea trout are always on the move in a flood. Some will be pushing further upstream and their places will be taken by more fresh fish in from the sea. Others just move around.

Eventually, at the end of the season, the upper river pools or upper loughs are always carrying the heaviest stocks. The pools and loughs further down will have their complement too waiting to run the small spawning side streams. It behoves the sea trout fisher to take good note of the effect of rising water and floods on the taking habits of sea trout. There are few better times to catch them than on falling water on the day after a flood.

LOCATING THE FISH

The primary consideration in fishing any lough is to fish the areas that hold fish and avoid wasting time in fishless areas. Success comes down to knowing the sea trout habits and the areas they frequent. Lough fishing can be divided into day and night fishing. Let's deal with the daytime fishing.

When fresh trout run into a lough, they move up straight away to the area around the mouth of the inflowing stream. If the stream leads to a lough further up, some of them will attempt to continue their journey if the water holds up. As the water drops, those that don't make it all the way will drop back to the lower lough. Therefore the first area to concentrate on and fish carefully is the delta around the mouths of inflowing rivers and streams. After a few days, the disappointed shoals begin to take up lies around the lake. These areas are quite specific and are governed by depth and the kind of bottom. The favourite depth seems to be between about five and fifteen feet (1.5–5m). Successful sea trout fishing is all about knowing the extent of these areas and where they are. Rocky mid-lake shallows, bays and the vicinity of islands are all likely places. This knowledge can only be gained by experience. This is where the services of a knowledgeable boatman come in. A boatman who is interested in his job has the fishing areas of a lough mapped out in his mind's eye. He knows exactly where to start a drift and when it should finish. It is a great skill and comes from years of experience. Every angler who engages in sea trout fishing must learn the hot-spots either from someone who knows them or by trial and error and the latter can take a lot of time. Small loughs are not so difficult to get to know but the big ones can take years.

Each area should be fished meticulously and quietly and the boat then moved on to fish the next one. When the last one is fished the process can begin all over again.

A number of things have to be borne in mind in regard to sea trout. The first is stealth and quietness. Anglers who know their lough and their sea trout fishing will map a given fish-holding area by reference to fixed points on the shoreline (bushes, rocks, etc.) and then fish it methodically in parallel drifts. At the end of each drift, the boat is quietly rowed up the water that has already been fished – often referred to by anglers as 'the dirty water'. The needless and careless use of outboard motors on a sea trout lough is an abomination and just one 'duffer' operating in a noisy and disturbing fashion can put the trout down and spoil the fishing for everyone over a wide area.

FISHING CONDITIONS

The right fishing conditions play a big part in successful sea trout fishing. For those who are fortunate enough to be able to choose the time and the day to go fishing, it is well to be able to read the signs. Obviously, the best time of year is when the sea trout are fresh in from the sea. The best conditions are a falling lake after a flood, moderate barometric pressure, a warm

but not hot day, a gentle wind and high cloud overhead. Sea trout thoroughly dislike extremes of heat, light, wind or barometric pressure and so fishing should be put off if there has been no rain for a long time, if the water temperature is excessively hot (20°C or over), if there is bright sunshine and no wind, or low hanging clouds giving a white milky light on the water, or a squally wind, or a rising lough, or thundery weather – to name but a few!

CHOOSING FLIES FOR SEA TROUT

Dictionaries of wet flies contain thousands of different patterns and dressings. To fish a sea trout lough successfully, it is necessary to have a range of wet fly patterns. But which ones? A casual observance of angling reports and fishing records tends to show that certain flies are mentioned more often than others and obviously these are the flies that caught the fish. However, one expert may claim that a particular fly is a killer. That may be so, fished by him on his lough and in his way. But for others, it may fail. The problem is that angling is not an exact science. In reaching conclusions in science experiments must be conducted and repeated in absolutely identical conditions. This is almost impossible in fishing because conditions are always so variable, and this will affect the behaviour of fish. All that we can be sure of are some general rules that long experience has shown to work in average situations.

Experience shows that claret, black, red, blue and silver are important components in sea trout flies. The following list should meet the requirements of most anglers and lough fisheries – Bibio, Black Pennell, Grey Ghost, Bloody Butcher, Blue Zulu, Bruiser, Camasunary Killer, Claret

Bumble, Claret & Mallard , Connemara Black, Daddy, Delphi Silver, Goat's Toe, Jacob's Ladder, Kingsmill, Silver Invicta, Raymond, Teal Blue & Silver, Bruiser, Watson's Fancy, Zulu and Red Ant (to be fished dry in the event of a fall of ants). I once heard Murt Folan of Galway, a veteran West of Ireland sea trout angler, state that the list could be reduced to a Bibio or Claret Bumble on the top dropper, a Watson's Fancy in the middle and a Black Pennell on the point. Perhaps the reason why we carry so many patterns is because of the mystery and the magic and the sense of the unknown that sea trout fishing exerts over its devotees. Part of the pleasure lies in pondering the possible effect that a change of flies might have on the sea trout's willingness to take. There are some successful anglers who claim that light conditions have a big bearing on the choice of flies and that a wet day calls for flies in which claret, silver and black predominate. A day with dense high cloud calls for predominantly black and silver flies. Clear water or bright weather calls for bright and silver flies. Loughs close to the tide call for flies with a touch of blue. An overcast sky and low cloud calls for a Bruiser. A very dark Claret Bumble is required at the end of the season. The advice is endless. No doubt all of it is good – on its day.

The size of the flies should be matched to the size of the wave and this can vary from size 8 in a big wave to size 14 in near calm conditions. Sizes 10 and 12 are used most often on a floating or intermediate line.

Normally, three flies are fished on a 6lb or 8lb (3x or 1x) leader. In a low ripple, I've found that two flies (size 14) and a 4lb (5x) leader gets better results. In a flat calm, there may well be a case for fishing only one, or a dry fly such as a small Sedge or Klinkhämer.

LOUGH STYLE

Of much more importance than pattern of fly is how the flies are fished. The most effective way is to cast a reasonably long line of some twelve to fifteen yards. The flies are retrieved in steady pulls till the water in which the leader was lying has been fished through. Another cast is then made, slightly to one side of the previous one. Sometimes the top dropper is worked along the surface. At other times the flies are worked deeper and drawn through the water and then lifted up out of it. Sometimes one method works and sometimes the other. And so it continues, fishing the water in a fan in front of the boat. The reason for only fishing the length of the leader is firstly because sea trout seem to take better at a distance from the boat. Secondly, the flyline seems to have a disturbing effect on them. I once knew an angler whose technique involved only allowing the leader to land on the water. He caught a lot of sea trout. When a trout takes, the best advice is to strike it positively on the take. And remember, sea trout are timid creatures. Always remain seated in the boat and avoid noisy movements or the splashing of oars.

TAKING TIMES

Sea trout sometimes respond to insects on the water, but this is a rare occurrence. Most sea trout 'rises' are quite independent of insect activity and they happen for reasons best known to the trout themselves. The rise occurs whenever they decide to come near to the surface and move about. Fresh run sea trout are more active than fish that have been in for a while. There is rarely much activity before ten in the morning but with luck it might last till lunchtime. The early afternoon can be a slack period. The four o'clock rise is eagerly anticipated and can continue sporadically till eight o'clock.

RED ANTS

It would be remiss of me not to mention the effect that a fall of red ants can have on sea trout. It's an unpredictable event which generally occurs in sultry, calm weather in August. Swarms of ants may get carried over the lough and fall on the water. To the sea trout, they are like manna from heaven and every trout in the lough comes to the surface to feast. At this time they will even rise right beside the boat. It is useful to have a small ant pattern to hand but failing that, in this situation they will take a small dry Sedge, Wickham's Fancy or even a small Kingsmill or Black Pennell (size 14) fished wet on a fine leader.

NIGHT FISHING ON THE LOUGH

This is one of the great angling experiences. Only the big trout seem to move at this time. I have never caught a finnock at night. July is the best month and the best evenings are so warm and windless that you must sprint to the boat to avoid the midges. Fortunately, biting midges rarely follow you on to the water. The lake should be flat calm or have a small ripple. It is best if there is no moon. The time to begin is about 10.30pm – never before. The trout move into shallower water and the areas of activity must be known. The boat is rowed gently to the chosen area and the oars are quietly shipped. The rise can last for ten minutes or it can continue till midnight. Then all activity ceases for about two hours – time to return to the lodge or guesthouse for a midnight cuppa. It starts again about 2am and lasts till the first light of dawn comes in the eastern sky – about 3am. It is then time to quit and make one's way wearily to bed.

Various fishing tactics can be employed. My preference is for a floating line and two wet flies on the leader. They are always a Silver Doctor and a Bloody Butcher, both size 10. Cast a long line and holding the rod tip low, make a very slow figure-of-eight retrieve. The take will be a solid affair, strong and determined. They rarely miss or come off when hooked. As the rise goes off, I let the flies sink for about twenty seconds before commencing the retrieve. This tactic often produces the biggest trout of the night.

Another tactic is to fish a dry fly – usually a big Sedge or a greased-up Muddler Minnow. It is retrieved slowly and the takes can be very violent.

It is only when you hook a big sea trout six feet down in black darkness that you really come to appreciate and marvel at the acuity of its vision. It is surely one of the most exciting experiences in flyfishing.

SEA TROUT FISHING IN THE RIVER

River fishing tactics are determined by the time of the year and the water conditions. In spring, a few rivers get a run of big spring sea trout. This occurs in April and the fish run on high water and with the spring tide at the time of the new moon.

The best fishing is on falling water with a floating or intermediate line and size 8 flies. Small salmon flies – Silver Doctor, Silver Stoat or Silver Rat – will suffice. During the day, the streams and pools are fished, wet fly style, paying particular attention to the quieter water where trout might be resting on their upstream journey. For evening fishing, right up till darkness falls, it is best to concentrate on the larger, deeper pools.

During the summer and into September, sea trout and finnock run in from the sea and forge upstream from pool to pool on falling water after every flood. Falling water usually only lasts for a few hours but it is a productive time. Wet fly fishing downstream is the normal tactic and a range of wet flies in shades of black, blue, silver and red – e.g. Black Pennell, Bibio, Silver Doctor and Watson's Fancy – in sizes 8 and 10 are usually reliable.

But there is another kind of daytime sea trout fishing that is done in the much longer, challenging periods between floods. For this, it is necessary to first identify where the shoals are resting. In between rises in water, the sea trout lie in the river pools. At least that is what they do in Connemara where I have experienced and witnessed some excellent daytime fishing. I have seldom found sea trout pools to be attractive places. In fact, they are often characterised by their dullness and lack of features. They have virtually no flow and without wind they can be mirror calm.

They must be approached with extreme care and caution. There should be no heavy foot falls, no hasty movements and no standing up close to the bank.

Tactics depend on the fishing conditions. If an upstream wind ripples the surface, begin at the bottom of the pool and using standard size 10 sea trout flies, cast across and slightly upstream. The casts should be short at first to fish the water close in and then the casts can become longer. The flies are retrieved as on a lough with the dropper in the surface or breaking through the ripple. When you have fished all the water within reach, quietly move a few yards upstream and begin again.

If there is no ripple on the pool, or a very slight one, and sea trout are observed moving, begin at the top of the pool, keeping low and well back. If there is bankside cover or trees, try to use them to prevent your silhouette standing out against the sky.

Your equipment will consist of floating line, fine leader and only two flies. Useful patterns are: Duck fly, Kingsmill, Bibio, Connemara Black and Black Pennell, lightly dressed in size 14. The cast is made and if there is any current in the pool, do not retrieve the flies but let the water carry them along. Where there is no movement, the flies are first allowed to sink slightly and a slow figure-of-eight retrieve is used. The best performance I ever saw by an angler using this method was by Danny Lydon of Galway who took fourteen sea trout to 3½ lbs from No-man's-land Pool at Ballynahinch in early August.

NIGHT FISHING ON RIVERS

July, August and early September are the prime months for night fishing. It is normally done on the bigger pools that are known to hold sea trout. Weather conditions play a big part and the best nights are those with little or no wind, warm and sultry. It is the kind of evening when the biting midges are out in force. There should be no moon.

If one is not familiar with the pool to be fished, it is best to do a recce during the day to become familiar with the conditions underfoot, bankside obstacles, overhead branches that are likely to snag a backcast, and so on. It is also useful to know a little about sea trout behaviour. Remember that at dusk some sea trout will move up to the neck of the pool and others drop back to the shallower water at the tail.

If the fishing expedition is to be successful, the first rule is that the pool should not be approached before darkness falls. A good rule of thumb is to approach only when the far bank fades from view. To do so sooner may well spoil a good night's fishing by frightening the trout.

To begin with, a floating line and two flies are used. My favourites are the same as those I recommend for the lough: the Bloody Butcher and the Silver Doctor, both size 10. No doubt others will favour different patterns. The flies are cast across the stream, the line is mended if necessary and allowed to swing around in the stream. They are then slowly retrieved up the slack water by the side of the stream and cast again. The takes are strong and sudden and a lot of fish are lost early in the night. The activity normally lasts till half an hour after midnight. If the terrain has been studied well in daylight, it can be profitable to move from the neck to the tail of the pool in the course of a fishing session.

Apart from your fishing tackle, there are other items that are essential. These include a small flash lamp, insect repellent, preferably a midge net to cover face and neck, landing net and possibly a small priest if the fish are not being returned.

ESTUARY FISHING

Estuary fishing for sea trout has been carried out for generations. The most common method was to use sand eels or mackerel strip. In recent times, flyfishing has become more popular. Indeed, Michael Rogan's Gadget was probably the original estuary sea trout fly. In testimony to its effectiveness, it is still used today.

There are many estuaries where sea trout can be fished with a fly. The estuaries of the Erne at Ballyshannon and the Moy at Ballina are particularly noted for the quality of their fishing. No doubt there are many others and my first experience of it was on the Owenduff Estuary in Co. Mayo.

In the estuary, we are fishing for feeding sea trout. This calls for somewhat different tactics to those employed on fresh water. To begin with, the rise and fall of the tides have to be taken into account. On big estuaries, when the tide is filling or full, the shoals of sea trout can be widely dispersed and notoriously difficult to locate. The hour before and after low tide can be most productive. Then the fish are confined to the main channel and easier to find.

Estuary fishing can certainly be dour from both the shore or from a drifting boat, but the use of a boat is tremendously helpful for it facilitates easy movement from one part of the estuary to the next. This is particularly true on the Moy Estuary. On the Erne Estuary, it would appear that at low tide it is more productive to beach the boat and fish from the shore or rather the edge of the sand bars. The boat has the effect of spooking the shoals, driving them ahead of it, whereas they can be more easily approached by careful wading along the beach.

The tackle used is much the same as on the lough: a single-handed rod, AFTM 7 or 8 line – floating and intermediate – six or eight pound leader and some flies which differ greatly from those used in fresh water. Most popular appear to be the streamer types, such as the Baltic Special, Parson Tom, White Lure, Black Lure and the Gadget. However, it is always well to seek and heed local advice. For instance, on the Owenduff Estuary, my most successful pattern has been a size 10 Camasunary Killer, but local anglers do well with the Teal Blue & Silver and Black Pennell. On one trip to the Owenduff, while I fished fruitlessly with small flies, a fellow angler took a 4lb sea trout on a large Black Lure.

There was little or no flyfishing for sea trout on the Moy Estuary until 1996 even though it was heavily fished with bait. The locals did not believe that sea trout would take a fly in the estuary. In August of that year, P.J. Nally and Willie McAndrew of Nephin Beg Angling Services and I set out to prove the theory wrong. We succeeded, landing over twenty sea trout to 14 inches on our first outing. Our biggest problem was locating the shoals on the broad, shallow flats. These were feeding sea trout that hit the fly with vigour. On that particular day, when the stomach contents were examined, they were found to be feeding on small shrimp or prawns. For those who wish to experience something of the excitement of a day's sea trout fishing, as might have been described by Kingsmill-Moore in the 1960s, I can think of no better place than the Moy Estuary in the company of P.J. Nally, Willie McAndrew or Judd Ruane of The Riverboat Inn, Ballina.

SOME FAVOURITE SEA TROUT FLIES

Because of the close relationship between sea trout and brown trout, and particularly in their feeding habits in fresh water, it is often possible to press brown trout flies into service and be successful. Mr T. C. Kingsmill Moore made an enormous contribution with his bumble patterns, especially for the top dropper for lough fishing. My inclination is to fish bright flies, with lots of silver, blue and red when sea trout are fresh. As the season progresses, more sombre shades (Claret & Bumble) and terrestrial imitations (the Daddy) do well.

Having said that, I am all too well aware of some of the lovely little flies that anglers fish on the East coast rivers and of course, our salt water fishing in the estuaries is still wide open for innovation and experimentation. That said, I have been wonderfully well served, over the years by the flies listed below.

CLARET BUMBLE

Hook: Size 8–12
Tying silk: Black
Rib: Oval gold tinsel
Tail: Strands of golden pheasant tippet
Body: Claret seal's fur – medium to dark
Hackle: A claret and a black cock hackle, palmered
Front hackle: Blue jay
This is one of the Kingsmill-Moore range of sea trout flies. It has yet to be equalled as a bob fly.

BIBIO

Hook: Size 8–14
Tying silk: Black
Rib: Fine oval silver
Body: Black, hot-orange, and black seal's fur
Hackle: Black cock palmered with another black cock hackle wound in front
The Bibio was the invention of Major Charles Roberts of Burrishoole. It comes second only to the Claret Bumble as a bob fly. There are some

that prefer to tie it with a centre section of red or claret seal's fur, although hot orange was the original colour.

WATSON'S FANCY

Hook: Size 8–12
Tying silk: Black
Rib: Fine oval silver tinsel
Tail: Golden pheasant topping
Body: Red seal's fur with black seal's fur in front
Hackle: Black cock
Wing: Crow wing slips
Eyes: Jungle cock
It is hard to equal the Watson's Fancy as a middle dropper fly, especially when the clouds are high and a west wind turns over a nice ripple.

GREY GHOST

Hook: Size 8–12
Tying silk: Black
Tail: Golden pheasant topping
Butt: Black ostrich
Rib: Fine oval silver tinsel
Body: Light grey seal's fur
Hackles: Black cock and grizzle cock,

117

palmered
Front hackle: Grey partridge or teal
This is not a fly that will stand out in your box, inviting you to tie it on. However, I find it an excellent choice for the middle dropper on a bright day or when there is a haze about and the light is bad.

BLACK PENNELL

Hook: Size 8–14
Tying silk: Black
Tag: Three turns fine oval silver tinsel
Rib: Fine oval silver tinsel
Tail: Golden pheasant tippetts
Body: Black floss
Hackle: Black cock
It is still difficult to recommend a more effective fly than the Black Pennell for the point (tail) fly position. It should be lightly dressed with the hackle fibres reaching well past the bend of the hook.

SILVER DOCTOR

Hook: Size 8–12
Tag: Fine oval silver
Tail: Golden pheasant topping
Butt: Red wool
Rib: Fine oval silver tinsel
Body: Flat silver tinsel
Hackle: Cambridge Blue cock
Wing: Bronze mallard with topping over
Head: Red varnish
I first tied this killing pattern for Michael Conneely, the Fishery Manager at Ballynahinch Castle Fishery in the early 1980s. It has served me well for night fishing ever since on both river and lough.

WILLIAM'S FAVOURITE

Hook: Size 12–14
Rib: Silver wire
Body: Black floss
Hackle: Black cock

In falling water or on the typical deep sea trout pool rippled by a good breeze, it is possible to catch sea trout on a range of lough flies like some of those listed above. However, in slow pools without a ripple, it is possible if sea trout are showing to take them on this fly, fished on a fine leader. It can make the difference between drawing a blank and taking maybe three or four good sea trout.

BALTIC SPECIAL

Hook: Size 8 longshank saltwater or silver plated
Tying silk: Red
Rib: Oval silver
Body: Flat pearl Lurex
Wing: Pearl crystal hair or mother-of-pearl Lureflash mobile under blue Lureflash mobile
Head: Red varnish
The Baltic Special is the first fly that comes to mind when I think of fishing sea trout in an estuary. It was the fly that cracked the sea trout on the Moy Estuary and for that alone, it deserves mention. Not only that, but it has caught a lot of fish since then. Some have had success with it on a floating line, but I prefer to fish it on an intermediate or even a fast sinking tip when the tide is in and the fishing is slow.

THE GADGET

Hook: Longshank saltwater sizes 8–4
Tying silk: Black
Rib: Fine oval silver tinsel
Tail and back: Slips of bronze mallard tied in at the end of the body with tips extending beyond the bend of the hook and the remainder brought over the top of the body – shellback style
Body: Flat silver tinsel over an underbody of grey floss silk
Head: A few turns of bronze peacock herl

SEA TROUT FLIES FOR RIVER AND LOUGH

TOP ROW Bibio, Williams' Favourite, Claret Bumble
MIDDLE ROW Grey Ghost, Watson's Fancy, Black Pennell
BOTTOM ROW Baltic Special, Silver Doctor

6

SALMON FISHING

The Atlantic salmon – *Salmo salar* – is a fascinating fish. It has inhabited Irish rivers for thousands of years, both as juvenile fish and as adults returning from the sea. Few fish are as well known. Stories of its life cycle, both mythical and real, have been related to successive generations of awe-struck children and the mystery of its coming and its going has been retold around many a fireside in days gone by when fish were plentiful and entertainment scant.

The salmon is an enigma, a riddle and a contradiction. When it comes back to the river after its sea journey, it does not eat, cannot digest food and it isn't hungry any more. It arrives back in the river from the rich feeding grounds of the ocean with enough energy stored in the fat of its muscles to last it for many months – even a whole year. When these facts are considered, it seems senseless that anyone should think of fishing for salmon by casting something into the water in the hope that they will eat it. Yet that is exactly what the salmon fisher does. The flyfisher must appear even more absurd because he or she is not even offering the fish some succulent tit bit, but a hook wrapped about with silk, tinsel, feather and fur. A lot of salmon fishers graduate from other forms of fishing and they continue in the mind-set that they are fishing for feeding fish. They give little thought to why they fish for salmon in the way they do.

WHERE DO WE BEGIN?

The mystery of why and how a salmon takes a fly lies in studying the fish itself. This research can be carried out by the angler, largely on the river bank, as he fishes. Like all research it should be carried out with an open mind, experimenting, observing and noting.

But always remember salmon fishing is not an exact science. Fishing conditions vary too much. We can only make general rules that can be applied in average situations. Like all anglers, the salmon fisher should learn not to be dogmatic in his pronouncements. The words 'never' and 'always' have no place in his vocabulary. Instead, salmon fishing could be regarded as something of an art. No two artists will paint a scene exactly the same. So it is with salmon fishing. It requires constant thought and study of the fish and the water it lives in and every salmon fisher must work out his own approach depending on the fishing situation in which he finds himself.

THE SALMON'S LIFE CYCLE

It all begins in about the month of December when the salmon lays its eggs in coarse gravel in the fast-flowing headwaters of a river. The winter frosts of January and February are just what's wanted to maintain a high level of dissolved oxygen in the water for the eggs to survive. The alevins, with their yolk sacks attached, hatch out in March, and come April or early May, the young fry are shoaling in the open river and competing for whatever food is available. They live in the river as parr for one or two years, at which point they change into silvery smolts and go to sea. The reason they go to sea is because of the inability of the river to provide for their food needs as they grow older and because of the abundance of food that the ocean can provide.

Self preservation is the salmon's primary instinct from the moment it leaves the gravel as a fry, and finding food is part of that. Young salmon, known as parr, are voracious little feeders. As any trout fisher can testify, one after another, they take the fly in the month of April as they make their way down river as smolts to the sea.

The smolts make their way to the rich feeding grounds of the North Atlantic where they remain feeding for one, two or more years. Those that return after one year are known as grilse or one sea-winter fish. They enter the river from late May to September and range in size from about 3-9lb. The late summer grilse may be bigger. Those that come back after two years are the spring fish or two sea-winter fish. They normally arrive between January and early May and weigh between 7 and 14lb. A few remain more than two years at sea and return as multi-sea-winter fish weighing 15lb or more.

Once the adult fish returns to the river, it ceases to feed. But for its entire life from the moment it became a fry, food and the search for food was one of its primary concerns. So strong was the instinct and the desire for food that it travelled thousands of miles to satisfy it. It is worth remembering this when we go fishing because the various food items it ate and what they looked like have an important bearing on the flies we choose and how we fish them.

As the salmon grows in freshwater, it shares the brown trout's menu according to the season: various nymphs, larvae, mayflies, olives, sedges, terrestrials, freshwater shrimp, worms, etc.

In the ocean, the seasons too determine its diet which ranges from the young of herring, cod, pollack, sandeels and capelin to krill, shrimps and prawns all of which are available in abundance in the North Atlantic, from the North Sea, to the coast of Greenland. So, during its life time, the salmon eats insects, crustaceans and small fish. The crustaceans (prawns, etc.) rate so highly in its diet that they account for the pink colour of the flesh.

It is a fact that the search for food was the only interest in its life from when it left the gravel of the redd till the days when it got ready to leave the ocean and return to the river of its birth. It is little wonder then that it

remembers this when it returns and can't resist taking food organisms into its mouth, even if it cannot eat or digest them. Most important of all, it is the salmon's memory of feeding that the angler relies on when he casts his fly and hopes for a take. It appears to be a logical conclusion. Our salmon is in the habit of feeding when the opportunity presents itself. Of course, there may be other reasons for taking a fly, like curiosity, aggression, even playfulness. But one of the strongest impulses has to be caused by the sight of something which resembles the kind of food it might be expecting to see at a given time and place.

HOW THE SALMON SEES

How any creature sees is determined by the kind of eye it has. Birds of prey have acute vision even at a long distance. Brown bears are short sighted. What of our salmon? It is the sight of the fly and not hunger that triggers a take. Much has been written about how salmon and trout see. It is possible that early authors reached incorrect conclusions, based on insufficient scientific knowledge. Some claimed that the salmon's eye was an inefficient,

second rate optical instrument; that an out of focus, distorted image was cast upon the retina and that it might see the general size, shape and colour of a fly but very little of the finer details. A more up to date point of view is that the salmon can focus from a short distance out from its eye to infinity and also across a wide field of vision due to the position of its eyes. In other words a salmon can see in almost every direction at once – except directly behind.

According to the literature, it can also focus on objects close up and experience tells us that it can see small objects. I can only conclude that our salmon's eye has evolved to see perfectly well in its watery world. In clear water we should never under-estimate its powers of vision. We have always to bear in mind that the salmon lives in a different medium to us. It is a swirling, watery environment, with the surface often broken by wind and ripple. Furthermore, it is denser than air, sometimes peat stained and often carries tiny particles of silt in suspension, all factors that would impair clear vision.

Salmon see through the surface of the water through a hole – called the cone of vision – which extends at an angle of about 48^0 all around them. Beyond the cone, the surface of the water acts like a mirror which reflects the bottom of the river and anything above it. If the water is rippled, it must look like a shattered mirror and the reflected image will be blurred. This has relevance for the angler in choosing the colour and size of his fly. In the first instance, when the fly is observed from below against the light, colour ceases to be important. It becomes a black object silhouetted against the sky. Secondly, when the fly is observed reflected in the mirror, if the surface is broken or rippled, and it usually is, then the fly cannot be seen clearly. Also it is the back of the fly that is seen – the top of the wing – and the fish will expect it to conform in colour, size and perhaps shape to whatever it is accustomed to seeing in that area.

And what if the fly is fished close under the surface so that it causes the water to hump over it? This creates a totally different image for the salmon to a fly fished three or four inches deep. There are many permutations and options. The angler has to learn all he can about them and bear in mind the light and water conditions as they may well influence the pattern of fly he chooses and the way he decides to fish it. For example, it is worth looking again at the traditional advice, 'a bright fly for a bright day'. It will be the wing of the fly which will be first seen by the fish, reflected in the mirror against the background of the river bottom. The brighter the day, the more illuminated the river bottom will be and a dark wing will stand out against it more clearly. And what of a shrimp fly with its translucent hackles? It has no wing and yet must be seen because it also takes a lot of fish. It soon becomes apparent that there are no hard and fast rules as to what fish can see because of the nature of the medium – water – and the surrounding environment. All we can be sure of is that the salmon's eyesight is adequate for its needs. When hunting and feeding, it relies on seeing its prey and it has done this successfully for a long time. We know

PREPARING THE LUNCH. Stoking the Kelly kettle on Lough Beltra with a spring fish on the bank

from experience that what we see and what our brain accepts are two entirely different matters. An eye, like a camera lens, sees everything because the eye passes the reflected light from everything to the retina. But we don't register every detail because the brain is incapable of accepting every tiny detail of what the eye has seen. And if this is the best we can do, how much less detail can the fish's small brain absorb of a fly? After all, it may only get a glance at it as it moves across the river. We are also told that a salmon's eye is sensitive to movement, which may explain why lightly dressed Irish shrimp patterns are so successful. All of these facts merit consideration when choosing a fly.

It follows that if the salmon's eye is so sensitive to movement, anglers must be careful how they approach a river and move about on the bank. Contrary to popular belief, salmon are easily scared and a quiet, stealthy approach is best.

WEATHER AND VISION

A fish's eye does not have eyelids, so it cannot close its eye or shade it in bright sunshine. Hence, on bright days in high summer, there is a much better chance of catching a fish in early morning or late evening than during the day. Anglers would do well to take heed of this and choose their fishing times accordingly. The unprotected eyes of the salmon can actually see much better in dull or fading light and small flies can be surprisingly effective in the late evening. I have seen several grilse caught on a size 16 as dusk faded to night.

On a bright summer's day with the occasional passing cloud, if one is preparing to fish a known lie for the first time, it is always better to wait for a cloud to pass over the sun. A five minute wait may feel like a long time when one is anxious to get the fly in the water but it is well worthwhile if it results in a hooked fish.

Something else worth remembering is that salmon face upstream in a river and into the wind on a lough to assist with breathing. When the sun is overhead or shining directly downstream, the fish with its lidless eyes will be blinded. The fisherman should note this and search out better options if they are available. One tactic is to wander along the bank and find a pool where the river meanders away from the sun. A better option is to find a pool or pools shaded by tall trees where the fish are feeling more comfortable. This very tactic helped me catch my biggest-ever salmon on an otherwise hopelessly bright day.

Colour and Salmon

Is colour important? Colour and pattern of fly probably causes more confusion and doubt than anything else.

If we are not catching fish, we wonder if it is because we have the wrong fly. As often as not, 'the wrong fly' means the wrong colour to the angler.

The experts tell us that there is no doubt that salmon can see and distinguish colours. It may well be that certain colours are more conspicuous to fish but in my opinion, salmon are not necessarily more attracted by one colour than another. We must approach this matter rationally. In the river as a juvenile fish and later in the ocean, the salmon feeds on prey that is mainly dull in colour, or black and white. Some is of neutral tone. Other prey is translucent and noticed only when it moves.

To avoid uncertainty and confusion, the thinking fisherman has to have an answer to the problem of colour but, unfortunately, until a salmon talks, there will be no answer except what experience alone tells us. Salmon are caught on dozens of different patterns and colours of fly every season. Each year, new patterns, combinations of colours – some outlandish – are added to the list and they too catch salmon. On any fishery, the fly usually in most demand is the fly that caught the last fish. Then when a fish is caught on a different fly, the demand suddenly changes. Flydressers will tell you that at salmon fisheries, there is often a 'run' on a particular fly every year. For instance it may be the fly that caught the first fish of the season. So why, I ask, should I worry unduly about the colour or pattern of the fly?

I have come to the conclusion that it is not the colour of a fly that

entices a salmon. The world of the salmon has mostly only drab shades and consequently vivid colours can have little meaning for the fish. I am therefore quite happy to fish with any pattern provided it is the right size and shape for the prevailing conditions. The fact that someone caught a salmon on a red fly in similar conditions yesterday is not a valid reason for putting on a red fly today. The question we must ask is 'was it the colour of the fly that attracted the fish or would any other pattern have been successful?' The answer is almost certainly that another fly would have been equally successful. I have seen it happen too often.

Not everyone will agree with me that the colour of a fly is of little importance; that the real skill in salmon fishing lies not so much in the colour or pattern of a fly but rather in its size, its tone and how it is fished relative to the water. But at least this approach resolves a problem that has created more self-doubt and confusion in salmon fishermen than almost any other.

THE LONG FAST

Some salmon spend a long time fasting in the river. They can arrive in late November or December and do not spawn till the following December.

More fish join them in the months that follow. They arrive, brimful of energy and live off the fat stored up in the muscles. They lie at the bottom of pools, resting and conserving the energy that they will require for the long journey to the redds in the headwaters and for the exhausting business of spawning.

Now every creature on this earth must sleep and rest to restore and conserve its energy and it appears perfectly reasonable that salmon should sleep too. Strangely, we never think of them as being asleep. We look at them with their eyes open – after all they cannot close them – and assume they are always awake. But this cannot be. Heavy, drowsy weather conditions seem to affect them much the same as us humans. I have no doubt they nod off to sleep. There are days when we know instinctively we are unlikely to catch a fish.

On the other hand, there are fresh, breezy days when we set out with high hopes of a fish, simply because of the weather. We have all watched anglers fish their flies down a pool like the Ridge Pool on the river Moy, covering hundreds of fish and not a single fish moves to take. The contrary can also be true and I have seen two or three anglers playing fish at the same time. It appears perfectly reasonable that salmon should sleep – and not always at night either.

So when are they awake and catchable? Once again, experience is a big help. We know that fresh fish in from the sea are more easily caught. They are active and restless, swimming around, jumping and splashing. Fresh fish run into the river on the rising water ahead of the tide. Some fisheries even display the times of the high tides on a daily basis to inform anglers fishing the lower pools on a river. There is also some evidence to suggest that fish in pools far up river also become active coinciding with the time of high tide.

Another occasion when fish are likely to be caught is when they are awakened by a rise in the water. They are usually caught for a short period as the river begins to rise. Later after the water reaches its peak and begins to fall, fish are caught when they are moving up from one pool to the next and after they have arrived to rest in a new pool. On spate rivers, it is well worth paying special attention to the tails of pools early in the day. Tired fish rest there after their early morning upstream exertions, before moving on.

Other factors likely to influence the taking times include a change in the air and water temperature or even a breeze to riffle the surface of a pool. It changes the oxygen content of the water and is likely to waken up sleeping salmon.

Any disturbance of the water is likely to get salmon moving. For instance, if a boat engine is driven over known salmon lies on a lough, salmon that have been comatose and unco-operative are likely to move and sometimes take a fly.

TEMPERATURE

Both water and air temperatures are factors in the life of a salmon. They will influence its time of spawning, metabolism and its upstream migration. On a cold spring day, a rise in the air temperature can often have the effect of making fish more active and likely to take a fly. A cooling breeze in summer can have a similar effect. Anglers would do well to take note of some of the more important effects of temperature on a salmon's behaviour.

For instance, in spring, salmon will not run far upstream or ascend weirs or falls until the water reaches 40°F (5°C). When the water temperature is between 40-48°F salmon tend to lie in the deepest part of a pool and will only take a big fly fished deep. When the water temperature exceeds 48°F, salmon are mainly taken on small flies fished close to the surface. It is now well established that water temperature affects the way a salmon reacts to a fly and this is something the angler should note well. Finally, once the temperature reaches 66°F (19°C) salmon become very lethargic and unresponsive.

At sea, the water temperature affects their feeding habits. Once again 48°F (9°C) seems to be the critical figure. In the cold water of winter, salmon feed mainly on small fish deep down and well away from the surface. As the surface of the ocean warms up and reaches the magical 48°F, a whole range of smaller food items like krill, prawns and shrimp become available and the salmon soon catch on to what is happening. These are all factors the salmon fisher should be aware of.

SALMON LIES

The first thing the salmon fisher must learn is where salmon lie in his river or lough. Salmon like to find comfortable lies in a river where they will rest on their upstream migration. The angler has to find these places if he is to show his flies to the fish. This can be done in either of two ways: by employing a local gillie who has learned them over several years or by fishing the river oneself for many years. The latter method can be slow and unsatisfactory for, to complicate matters further, the places that salmon lie in a river can change as the water in the pools rises and falls and gravel beds shift. However he does it, the angler must get to know exactly where salmon lie if he is to concentrate his efforts in the right places.

READING THE WATER

A river is a complex place with a lot of variety, unlike a canal where there is a great sameness and uniformity of depth, speed and the character of the bottom and sides. The distribution and number of the salmon lies is determined by topographical factors: varying gradient, width, depth and the nature of the river bed and banks. These factors create different types of water: falls, white water, riffles, runs, streams, glides, flats, backwaters, pools and so on. Each has its own speed of current and type of bottom – gravel, rocky, boulder strewn, sandy or silty. As the river rises and falls, the depth and speed and strength or 'push' of the water changes. One of the first skills the salmon fisher must learn is an ability to read the water. We call it rivercraft or watermanship. It is on this skill that the angler relies to help him fish the fly properly.

The salmon lives in a different medium from us and has lots of experience of assessing the various speeds of the water. It is not only aware of the current but uses it at all times. It is also aware of all the other creatures that share the river. It has caught and fed on many of them. It has a lot of experience of assessing the speed at which they move and how they move according to their size. It knows that everything which is not drifting downstream at the speed of the river, but is holding its station or swimming about is a living thing.

WATER SPEED

This is where the angler has to begin to understand the salmon and, instead of thinking like a land animal, he must begin to think like a fish. Our inclination is to judge the speed of the fly that we cast to the far side of the river and watch it swinging around to our bank, relative to the bank and the bottom of the river. But as far as the salmon is concerned, it judges the speed of anything swimming in the river, against the speed of the current, and not against something stationary like a boulder or the river bank or bottom. If a fly is moving at 2mph relative to the bank, we consider it is moving slowly. But from our fish's perspective, if it is moving at 2mph against a current flowing at 8mph, then its water speed is 10mph. Alternatively, if a

PRECIOUS PARR
The 'fingerprint' markings of the young salmon distinguish it from its trouty cousins. The parr's memory of its freshwater feeding habits may very well influence its taking habits when it returns to the river as a mature salmon.

130

Fresh from the sea and in prime condition this springer is ready for the long fast that it will endure during its time in freshwater. Tailers like the one in this photo are little used nowadays, most anglers favouring the net. But if you are intending to release the fish you are better off with neither

fly is being stripped fast downstream at 10mph in a stream flowing at 8mph, its true speed relative to the water and the fish is only 2mph. The angler must develop water-sense and learn to judge the speed of the fly relative to the water. There are other factors to be taken into account too if the angler is to attract fish to his fly. A small fly must have a slower water speed while a big fly is fished faster. The salmon has lived all its life in the river and the ocean and is well aware of the speed at which creatures of different sizes can swim. If the fly is moving too fast, it appears unnatural and if it appears unnatural, the salmon will not take it. In fact, it may even be frightened and put off from taking for some time.

FLY SIZE

The salmon displays an unusual ability to make distinctions in the size of fly it will take. In spring, when the water temperature is below 48°F, it generally will only take big flies of three to six inches in length and fished deep. When the water warms up, salmon are taken on small flies, right down to size 16s and fished close to the surface.

So, choosing the size of fly is related to water temperature and to how the fish must have fed earlier in its life. In low temperatures at sea, large food items (mostly small fish) were only available deep down. As the ocean warmed in spring, small food items (shrimps, squid, krill) became more plentiful near the surface. In fresh water in summer, it fed as a parr on insects of various kinds. The salmon fisher has to be aware of these facts and how they affect the fish's taking habits. Thus, salmon can be caught on 6-inch Collie Dog tube flies in early spring, and in summer they will take a tiny Blue Charm or even a trout fly, e.g. Green Peter. They may sometimes take a big fly in summer, but they are very unlikely to take a tiny fly in spring when the water temperature is below 48°F. After all, you don't see many insects about when it is that cold. Fly size in water over 48°F (9°C) can vary from about 1¼ inches long (size 4 single) to a size 16 double – depending on the water conditions.

So critical is the temperature mark of 48°F (in high water some say it is 50°F) that anglers often carry a thermometer in spring to test the temperature. They can then judge when to fish a big fly on a sunk line or when to fish the fly closer to the surface. It is only by using a thermometer that one can with certainty decide on fly size in spring. You would be surprised how many degrees the water temperature can vary during the course of a day's fishing in response to factors like snowmelt, a prolonged period of sunshine or a sharp rise in the air temperature.

WHAT THE SALMON FLY REPRESENTS

Why does a fish that does not eat in freshwater take a fly? Every fisherman has to find his own answer to this perplexing question. For me, it could be that on its return from the sea, after a period of voracious feeding, the instinct to attack and kill its prey still remains. It could also be that it will take the fly out of a feeling of playfulness, curiosity or even aggression.

Now salmon flies are strange looking assortments of hair, feather, tinsel, silk and iron. Most of them look like nothing in nature and with the availability of modern materials, they are getting stranger looking every day. Yet, thousands of salmon are caught on these unlikely looking creations. To me, it seems unlikely that the salmon examines them very carefully and the fact that it will take a fly better in broken swirling water may offer another clue. Perhaps the salmon doesn't see their detail very well but rather is attracted by how the fly moves. We know the salmon's eye is quick to spot movement. If this is so, then the fly becomes an illusion of something that the fish expects to see in this situation. Most likely the fish doesn't see the fly as an exact imitation of something living but rather its size and movement creates the illusion of an indistinct creature and the fish is attracted to it. The angler must endeavour to maintain this illusion of life and he can do so by controlling the movement of the fly with rod and line. The only thing that will destroy the illusion is unnatural movement or if the size of fly is seriously wrong. In low clear water, a big fly, fished slowly, ceases to be an illusion and the fish sees it for what it is – an artificial fly. When this happens, it is time to try a smaller fly or speed up the retrieve.

The big sunk fly (Collie Dog, Willie Gunn, etc.) represents a small fish and the colour of the fly seems to have little effect on the willingness of the salmon to take. A black or dark fly is more easily seen in clear water and a brightly coloured one in peaty or opaque water.

With the small fly in summer, matters are different. Most probably, it does not represent a fish. Instead, it may remind the salmon of the types of food to which it was accustomed in the river or lough as a juvenile fish, or the plentiful food types near the surface of the ocean as it warmed up in late spring and summer. Hence, our small flies create the illusion of nymphs, pupae, hatching mayflies, sedges, daddys and terrestrial insects – or perhaps small marine shrimps, prawns and krill. And so in summer we fish near the surface with a variety of small flies such as strip-winged and hair-winged flies, Goslings, Green Peters, Daddies, Bibios, various shrimp flies and mini-tubes, and salmon are taken on all of them.

FISHING THE BIG SUNK FLY

We know a little about the salmon and its food in cold, ocean water and we must now find out the best method of presenting the fly in early spring. The secret of success lies in fishing it at the right depth and at the right speed. The colder the water, the deeper you must fish and the speed at which you fish must always be judged relative to the speed of the water and not against anything stationary like a rock. Depth is achieved by using sinking or sink-tip lines, fast sinking leaders and heavy flies, depending on water speed and depth. The speed at which your fly moves should be equal to the speed at which little fish swim, namely 2–3mph and they may strug-

gle and drop back in fast water. At times the small fly can be made to dart away by the angler, as if afraid of being eaten by a bigger fish. All this gives an appearance of life to a well-fished fly. The whole secret of fishing a big fly well in cold water is getting the depth and the speed right.

SUMMER FISHING

By 'summer fishing', I'm referring to the tactics employed to fish for salmon once the water temperature rises above 48°F (9°C). This usually involves fishing with a floating line, but not always. For instance, on the river Lackagh in Co. Donegal, local experts insist on the use of a sinking line till the end of June – irrespective of water temperature. Salmon can be perverse creatures and it is always well to seek and heed local advice.

In circumstances of high, fast water, a sink-tip or intermediate line may be required to prevent the fly from skating.

Everything changes once the water temperature rises. The angler who understands this and the effect it has had on the salmon all through its life knows that different fishing tactics are now called for when fishing the

ABOVE
Tiny waters, such as this stretch of the river Sheen, near Kenmare in Kerry can hold good salmon. These are conditions for 'dibbling' the fly.

RIGHT
Tense moments: a salmon comes to the net

134

small fly. We have just looked at the situation when the water is cold and the salmon feeds on small fish. In the warmer weather of spring and summer an astonishing transformation takes place in both freshwater and in the ocean. Food is suddenly in plentiful supply, both aquatic and terrestrial. Our fish begins to look upwards and move more frequently near the surface. No doubt, even though it cannot eat when it returns to freshwater, it is reminded by the milder weather and longer days of the weeks and months when food was plentiful, easy to see, easy to catch and near the surface. It is up to the angler now to choose different flies and the ways of presenting them that will create the correct illusion or image to entice a fish to look up and take it. Whether it is motivated out of aggression, curiosity, playfulness or most likely the memory of how it used to feed, is of no great concern to the angler. All he is concerned about is enticing the fish to take the fly.

Flies for summer salmon fishing are tied on either single, double or treble hooks and small tubes. The range of sizes is roughly size 8–16 in trebles; size 8–16 in doubles; and size 4–12 in singles. Occasionally in high water, a big fly like a Collie Dog is pressed into service and on its day, can produce a fish too. It is not necessary to carry a lot of different patterns but it is essential to have them in a range of sizes down to the smallest. In general, fast flowing rivers need bigger flies and low flow calls for smaller ones.

In choosing a suitable fly, the fisherman should concern himself with size and shape and above all, the way it behaves in the water. As to the colour, I personally do not think it really matters. Let each fisherman fish with the colour of fly that pleases him! The skill in fishing lies not in the colour of the fly but in the illusion that it creates and the way that it is fished. Once it moves in the way the fish expects it to move, almost any pattern will do.

FISHING THE FLY IN SUMMER

We have all heard the advice 'Let the water fish the fly'. If ever there was a recipe for failure, this is it. Fishing a small fly properly is all about controlling it with the rod and line to present the best possible illusion to the fish. Letting the water fish it will cause it to do some crazy things, many of which are not likely to attract salmon and some may positively frighten it.

There are many ways of presenting a fly to a salmon – from the front, from the side or even from the rear. Presentation is governed by the kind of water being fished, the shape of the fly, etc. and in certain situations, more than one kind of presentation can elicit a take. Salmon seem to react well to any form of presentation which causes the fly to move towards the fish. The fly should approach the salmon at a controlled speed, and the speed should emulate that of a creature of similar size. Every part of the river that holds fish must be covered and every cast should be fished thoughtfully and carefully. As mentioned earlier, a river will have many currents and swirls and eddies, all mingling and changing in both speed and direction, depending on the gradient and the topography of the bottom and of the banks.

If a line is cast across a current or stream, the line is dragged into a big curve or 'belly'. The result is a 'dragged' fly which comes over the fish at too great a speed. The speed of a dragged fly can be corrected and controlled by 'mending' the line (see page 177). Mending the line is done with an oval movement of the rod tip immediately after the cast has been completed. The curve formed in the line is thrown over – without pulling on the fly – so that the downstream belly becomes an upstream curve. This has the effect of reducing the pressure on the line and allowing the fly to move across the river slowly in a more natural fashion. Alternatively, if the river is flowing slowly, a downstream mend may be necessary to speed up the fly and give it a resemblance of life.

FLY PRESENTATION OPTIONS

There are as many ways of presenting a fly to a salmon as there are currents in a river. All of them challenge the angler to be observant and thoughtful and to fish the fly in the way the fish expects a creature of that size to move (relative to the kind of water it is being fished in). As a general rule, a salmon responds better to a fly moving towards it than away from it. It does not like to be asked to expend energy. Try to make it easy for it to take the fly. Incidentally, a fish is unlikely to come up more than about eight feet to take a fly in river or lough.

The norm is to fish one fly on the cast, except in special circumstances, such as 'backing up' when most anglers fish two. But nothing is written on stone and I know an angler who always fishes two flies and catches the majority of his salmon on the dropper.

On a river where the current is flowing steady and true, the angler begins at the top of the pool and fishes down. The line is cast down and across at an angle of 45° to the bank and fished back to his own side. It is a rare situation where some adjustment of the line does not have to be made when fishing down and across. When the cast is made and the line settles on the water, the rod tip follows the line and eventually finishes pointing downstream along our own bank. The fly ceases to move effectively as soon as it reaches the slack water on our own side. Immediately, a few yards of line should be retrieved by hand before making the next cast. This should be done carefully as there is no accounting for how or when a salmon will take. Nor indeed, should we assume that they all lie facing upstream. They always lie facing the current and in a back-eddy that may mean a fish is facing in a downstream direction.

Even when fishing 'down and across' in order to take account of the variations in the flow all the way across the river, the angler will need to make constant adjustments to the line in order to control the movement of the fly. This means slowing it down here, speeding it up there, allowing it to drop back somewhere else in faster water and so on. Salmon fishing calls

for constant reading of the water. Remember, a fly that is merely holding station in a current flowing at 3mph is – from the fish's point of view – perceived to be swimming at 3mph.

If fish are lying in slack water on the far side of a stream, it is a mistake to mend the line right after the cast is made. This only causes the fly to sink, in which case it loses all semblance of life and become just another piece of debris. Instead, the current should be allowed to put a belly in the line to move the fly quickly through the slack water and the line is only mended when the fly reaches the faster water.

BACKING UP

Of course not every salmon river will lend itself to fishing 'down and across'. Some salmon-holding pools barely move at all when the water drops. This calls for different tactics if fish are to be caught. In 'backing up', instead of the angler starting at the top of the pool, he begins at the bottom. The fly is cast across and slightly upstream. The angler then takes a few steps upstream and he begins to strip in the line quickly. This tactic, popular on rivers like the Erriff, works best with an upstream wind rippling the surface of the pool and it is always performed using a single-handed rod and usually with a sinking or a sink-tip line.

Another method of fishing slack water, when the surface is broken by a ripple, is to fish it as one would fish a lough. This involves using two flies and casting with the wind. The rod tip is then raised and the dropper fly

Sea lice
*An indication
that the salmon
has only just
come in from the
sea. After a few
days in
freshwater these
parasites drop
off.*

(usually a Black Pennell or a Bibio) is worked along the surface.

If fish are known to lie in very fast flowing water, perhaps at the head of a run, they can be caught by 'dibbling' a fly on the surface just over the lie. To do this, it is necessary to use two flies. The rod is held over the stream, the point fly acts as an anchor and the dropper fly 'tips' the surface of the water like a pendulum. The constant tipping action appears to have the effect of provoking the fish to take. In Ireland, the term for this technique is 'tipping the fly'.

I was first introduced to 'mini-tube' fishing by Robert Gillespie of Foxford. This method involves fishing small tube flies in either streamy water or in slower water that is rippled by the wind. The mini-tube is fished close to the surface but it should not skate. By careful control of the tension on the line, the water 'humps' over the back of the tube fly. This has a fatal attraction for spring salmon (in water over 50°F) and grilse in summer.

METHODS OF WORKING AND RETRIEVING THE FLY

Different fly types call for variations in how they are worked and retrieved. This has to do with the kind of illusion we want to present to the fish. Large flies (tubes, Waddingtons, etc.) of over three inches are usually fished to represent little fish. We know that small fish normally swim at about at 1–2 mph, but when they are frightened – say by the sight of a large predator – they will dash away suddenly for a yard or two before swimming slowly again. The big fly ought to imitate this movement.

Irish shrimp flies, lightly dressed, give a good representation of the shrimps and prawns that our fish found so nourishing and attractive when it was feeding at sea. These tiny, translucent creatures move about in leaps and darts and it is their movement that usually first attracts attention. The artificial should be fished with a jerky movement to give the illusion of life.

There is a uniquely Irish method of fishing these flies that seems to increase their effectiveness. The fly is cast more squarely across the current than is usually considered acceptable. The rod tip is held high and 'tipped' or 'jigged' (imparting an up and down movement) in a controlled fashion and this action is transmitted to the fly, causing the hackles to pulse.

Hairwinged flies, strip winged flies and hackled flies are likely to represent anything – pelagic, aquatic or even terrestrial. Provided the size is right and they are fished properly relative to the water, they will all take a fish. I especially like to fish a hairwing fly in a smooth glide, casting it down and across and letting it swing quietly and smoothly without any movement of the rod tip.

Then there are the imitative patterns such as the Daddy, Green Peter (imitating various sedges), Gosling and Bibio, which represent insects that fish were accustomed to when they lived as juveniles in fresh water.

No one knows what exactly goes on in the mind of the salmon, but it is safe to assume that it is very aware of what is going on around it. Hence there are times and places where these flies can cause our fish to make one move too many, leading to a fatal mistake.

HOOKING A SALMON

What should you do when a salmon takes the fly? It is a question that has probably been around for as long as man has fished the fly. Even the 'experts' give conflicting advice. There is no single answer because salmon have different ways of taking that require different responses. For the most part we don't even see the take and hence are unprepared to respond. In short, we will never land all the fish that take. We will hook some and we will lose some, as is the case in all forms of flyfishing. There is no simple answer to the problem.

My best advice is to avoid any form of reaction or striking when the take is first felt. For best results, do nothing. A lot depends on being alert and how we regard the fish. My way of thinking is to consider that here is a fish that is accustomed to taking hard things (shrimps and prawns) into its mouth and crunching them. So it is not going to spit the fly out quickly. Furthermore, to get a deep hook-hold I must let the fish turn away with the fly. Consequently, when fishing a floating line, I try hard not to react, not to tighten the moment I feel a take. I usually hold a loop of line trapped by the index finger against the rod handle and I release a yard or two at the first sign of a take, dropping the rod tip at the same time. Then I hold the fish tight momentarily to set the hook before getting it on the reel and starting to play it.

When fishing a sunk flyline I don't usually give line on the take.

Instead I just hold tight, without reacting, and usually the fish hooks itself.

PLAYING A SALMON

Once the salmon is hooked, the rod tip should be held high and the first priority is to get any loose line wound on to the reel if the fish hasn't already taken it. If wading, try to keep as much line as possible out of the water and when the fish is under control, retreat nearer the bank where the water pressure is not so great. After that, playing a salmon is essentially about keeping the leader and line away from snags and gradually wearing down the fish.

Eventually you get ashore or if the fish is hooked from the bank the next move is to try and get the fish up-river away from the tail of the pool. Staying well back from the bank, exert as much pressure as you judge appropriate and 'walk' the fish up towards the top of the pool. Here it is played out, preferably in quiet water, by being kept on the move using side strain and only brought into shallower water when it begins to weaken. Don't try to bully or haul a salmon in too soon.

In the end it will relent and be netted or tailed by hand. It pays to be especially careful with big fish when they begin to tire. The place for landing them should be decided well beforehand. It should preferably have an ample back-water and the fish should always be netted or slid ashore facing downstream. It is a mistake to allow a big, tired fish back out into a strong stream. Unable to swim against the current, it will be swept away, and unless you can follow it and find another suitable back-water, you may well lose the fish. It is always best to anticipate such an eventuality towards the end of the fight and at the first sign that it may be heading out into the stream, quickly and deftly apply side-strain.

SALMON ON THE LOUGH

Every season, hundreds, if not thousands of salmon are taken on Irish loughs, many of them on the fly. Indeed some lough fisheries are 'fly only'. The fishing is done from drifting boats. Salmon lies on a lough are very precise and sometimes a mere boat-length to either side can make the difference between success and failure. The first priority is to know the areas where fish lie. This knowledge comes only with experience and few people have a better knowledge than the local boatman who fishes the lough and gillies the anglers in all seasons and weather and water conditions. Fish will be in both rocky areas and on the edge of sandy beaches and are catchable in about 4–8 feet of water. For success, the water must be rippled – a small ripple will do and, as in the river, most fish are caught when they are active. This activity can be initiated by a rise in water, but more often, a slight change in air temperature, light conditions or even the direction and strength of the wind.

In spring, when the water is cold (below 50^0F) the practice is to fish big flies on a sinking or sink-tip line. The size of fly used is normally a size

4 or size 6 and they are usually dressed on single hooks – Curry's Red Shrimp, Hairy Mary, etc. Occasionally, big tubes are used with success but they are difficult to cast. When the temperature rises, the size of fly gets smaller – from size 6 to 16 – depending on the conditions. A variety of flies may be used and I have found a Green Peter to be one of the best.

Intermediate and floating lines are used. In recent seasons, the clear Aircel intermediate and the Cortland sink-tip lines have been particularly popular. As with river fishing, timing the setting of the hook is critical. Certainly any form of snatched striking is out of the question. Usually all that is required is a dropping of the rod tip to let the fish turn down, followed by a firm tightening of the line to set the hook. After that, the fish is manoeuvred down wind, behind the boat and played out.

SALMON TACKLE FOR RIVER AND LOUGH

The leader should be thick enough not to break off when fishing a big fly and yet thin enough to allow a small fly to swim attractively. The range of breaking strains is therefore from about 25lb down to 6lb. In very clean water, clear, fine monofilament is best as there is some evidence that fish may be shy of heavy or dark leaders.

For flylines, I use only floating and sink-tip lines, with a fast sinking braided leader, if thought necessary. I never use a full sinking line. The lines can range from AFTM 12 to 7 depending on the size of flies being fished and the wind conditions.

Fly reels are basically line containers. When salmon fishing, they should be big enough to hold the flyline and plenty of backing – a length of at least 150 yards.

For fly rods, it helps to have a choice of one or two different lengths. As a minimum requirement, you should equip yourself with two rods: a double-handed rod and a single-handed rod. The length of each is very much a matter of personal choice, 12-15 foot for the big rod and 9-11 foot for the single-handed rod.

As stated elsewhere, when selecting an outfit, the wisest method is to have someone help you whom you know is competent. This is especially true when selecting a double-handed salmon rod. Quite apart from the cost – and it can be substantial – the primary consideration should be that it has a good action and be a joy to fish with. A rod with a progressive action is less tiring. This means that when casting it you should be able to 'feel' the action all the way back down to the butt. A good rule of thumb is to take the butt section, hold it at eye level, with the hands approximately 3 feet (1m) apart with fingers on top and the thumbs underneath. Then try to flex it. If it flexes fairly easily, it is a good sign. However, if the flexing requires a lot of effort, put it aside and search out one that flexes more easily.

For those who like to carry a landing net, it should be at least 2 feet in diameter with a quick release shoulder strap. It is also a good idea, in case of necessity, to learn to land a fish by hand.

RIGHT
The flyfisher's ultimate prize: a spring salmon. This one, a fourteen pounder from Delphi, was caught by Franz Schäfer of Munich

142

WHERE THE SALMON LIE IN THE RIVER

Salmon will take up positions in a river which satisfy some very specific requirements. Energy conservation is one of them and the salmon in particular, which ceases to feed in freshwater and has a long journey upstream, looks for resting places that will not exhaust it.

Obstructions in the pools such as a boulders and rocks, groynes, weirs and bridges – all these will attract fish. But salmon can also take up station in the most unexpected places: shallow runs, tucked in close to the bank, directly in front of boulders where there may be relief from the full force of the current.

The experienced angler will learn to identify these holding lies and concentrate his casts around them.

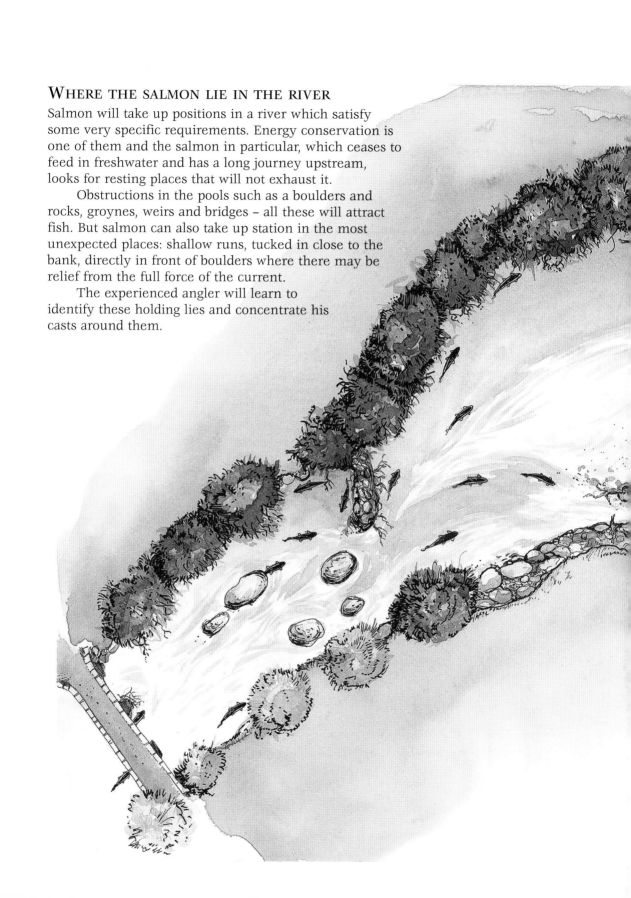

WHERE TO FIND TROUT IN A RIVER

Unlike the salmon, a trout is always on the look-out for food, so it will be found in places where the foodstream can be watched, where it feels safe and where it can conserve energy.

River trout are most visible to the angler when they are rising to insects trapped on the water surface. The insects are carried downstream with the current and the trout will take up position where they can see and take these morsels without risking attack from predators. Again, boulders, weeds, submerged objects in the river – these are likely places to find trout. But because they are usually smaller and better camoflaged than the mature salmon they can be found in parts of the river that might appear too shallow or exposed to accommodate a fish.

FAVOURITE SALMON FLIES FOR IRISH RIVERS

The salmon fisher should give more thought to size of fly, how it is tied and the depth and manner of its movement than to colour and pattern. I would not claim to be a 'one fly' fisherman. However, equipped with the following flies in a range of sizes, I would feel prepared for most situations.

COLLIE DOG

Wing: Black hair from the point of a dyed black squirrel tail or black goat hair (2-5" or 6.5cm-12cm long)
Body: Aluminium, plastic or copper tube ranging in length from ¾" to 3". The copper tube is usually wrapped with flat or embossed silver tinsel.
Hackle: Red dyed beard hackle

I have no hesitation in listing the Collie Dog as my favourite salmon fly on rivers and it should not be discounted on the loughs either. I have caught salmon with it in all seasons, from Delphi to Castleconnell, Erriff and Moy, not forgetting one rare early-season fish from the Dee (Co. Louth) on 11 February. It is just so effective. I recall taking two springers at Castleconnell on a day when the two other rods sharing the beat, blanked despite using both spinner and worm. In 1998, a remarkable 206 salmon and grilse were taken on it at Delphi. Nor is there any great mystery about how it should be fished. All you need do is tie it on, cast it to the far side of the river and let it swim back across the current. In late summer and September, if fish are dour, cast it square across the river and strip it back quickly. In this case, use a long aluminium tube – up to 3" – and a long goat hair wing. When fished deep, it should be tied on a 1-2" copper tube overlaid with embossed silver tinsel. For summer fishing, my preference is to tie it on a ¾" or 1" aluminium or plastic tube.

It should not be overlooked on the lough either where it is best fished on an intermediate line. Numerous fish have fallen to it in Fin Lough including the 1999 season's best fish of 16lbs taken by Michael Hayes of Dublin.

For myself, I like to tie the smaller ones (2-3" long) with hair from the point of a black squirrel tail. If you can find a tail which has hair that is kinked or wavy, so much the better, as this makes a particularly attractive fly with a wonderful action in the water.

VAMBECK SPECIAL

Hook: Size 12 single or double
Tying silk: Black
Tag: Fine oval silver tinsel
Rib: Fine oval silver tinsel
Tail: Golden pheasant topping
Body: Flat silver tinsel
Hackle: Black cock
Wing: Black squirrel tail
Eyes: Jungle cock

Nearly everyone will agree that the Silver Stoat's Tail is a great salmon fly. Louis Vambeck of Mullingar took the original, added Jungle Cock eyes and, I believe, made it an even better fly. Louis considers that pale cream Jungle Cock eyes are more effective than the white or deep orange ones. I have had numerous successes with it both here and in Scotland, fishing it in clear water on both floating and intermediate lines. My favourite sizes are 8-12, always dressed on double hooks.

SALMON FLIES

TOP ROW *Curry's Red Shrimp, Foxford Shrimp*
2ND ROW *Vanbeck Special, Beltra Badger, Green Peter*
3RD ROW *Black and yellow mini-tube, Silver Petticoat*
Yellow tube
Collie Dog

THE MINI-TUBE

Tube: 1/2" x 2mm plastic tube
Tying silk: Black
Tag: Fine oval silver
Rib: Fine oval silver
Body: Black tying silk
Wing: Yellow and black bucktail, tied in quarters
Hook: Size 16 treble (Partridge X1BR) except in fast water where a size 14 treble may be needed to prevent the fly skating. Only Partridge X1BR hooks are suitable as they allow the fly to swim at the correct depth.

'Piscator non solum piscator' or there's more to fishing than catching fish, to paraphrase the Latin poet. It should be fun too. I know of no better way of having fun with salmon than by fishing a mini-tube when the conditions are right. They come in all shades and colours but I only ever use a black and yellow. I don't know of any other method of flyfishing for salmon that gets so many responses. They don't all take hold at the first attempt but persistence is often rewarded. The mini-tube works a treat with fresh fish – whether spring fish or grilse – when the water is clear and the temperature is 50°F or more. It is effective in streamy, riffled water, fast glides or even still pools when rippled by the wind. For best results, cast the fly over known lies and allow it to fish around causing a slight wake (or figure-of-eight it back through the ripple, against the wind). The fish will chase the fly, apparently investigating this intruder in their living space. The takes come irregularly – sometimes at the first attempt, but more often at the second or third. Be patient. Refrain from lifting the rod till the fish pulls hard. Only then should you react in the normal way for the floating line – by setting the hook. It would appear that it is the wake, or the water humping over the mini-tube, that attracts the fish. But it is impera-tive that your fly does not skate. For this reason, the angler must control the fly relative to the current. This means keeping it in view. I prefer to fish it on a single-handed rod. The small hooks take a remarkably good hold and invariably forceps are required to remove the hook.

THE YELLOW TUBE

Tube: 2–3" long
Wing: Yellow or lemon yellow dyed bucktail

When the river is high and coloured, particularly in the spring, when most anglers are spinning, I like to think that the fish can see and take the fly too. I have great confidence in these conditions when I am fishing a big yellow fly like the Yellow Tube.

FOXFORD SHRIMP

Hook: Sizes 6–14 single, double or treble
Tag: Oval silver tinsel
Tail: Golden pheasant red breast feather
Rear body: Black seal's fur
Rib: Oval silver tinsel
Middle hackle: Silver badger cock
Front body: Fiery brown seal's fur
Rib: Fine oval silver tinsel
Wing: Jungle cock roofed, or as eyes on the smaller sizes
Front hackle: Ginger cock
Head: Red

When it comes to shrimp flies, it is hard to single out just one as being a favourite. The Bann Special, Claret Shrimp, Yellow Shrimp – all have served me well and I will always carry them all in a range of sizes. However, when the conditions look difficult, the water is perhaps dropping away and bordering on being too low, I'll put on a Foxford Shrimp. It brings back sweet memories and has scored some spec-tacular 'late goals' for me on both Irish and Scottish rivers.

FAVOURITE SALMON FLIES FOR THE LOUGH

BELTRA BADGER

Hook: Sizes 4–10, single or double
Tag: Fine oval silver tinsel and yellow floss
Tail: Golden pheasant topping
Butt: Black ostrich herl
Rib: Oval silver tinsel
Body: Flat silver tinsel
Hackle: Lemon yellow from the second turn of the tinsel
Throat: Cambridge blue or pale Kingfisher blue
Wing: Badger hair with a few fibres of red bucktail underneath and a topping over all
Head: Black

This has to be one of the greatest of salmon flies for lough fishing. It has been my first choice for the dropper for spring salmon fishing at Lough Beltra and Finlough for twenty years. I know it works well for others too from the number of requests I get to tie it.

GREEN PETER

Hook: Sizes 8–12, bronze hook
Rib: Fine oval gold tinsel
Body: Green seal's fur
Wing: Four slips of hen pheasant secondary tied in flat, to lie low over the body
Hackle: Best quality red game

If the Beltra Badger is my first choice for spring fish, the Green Peter rates equally highly for grilse. It is very effective – probably because it arouses memories for the fish of their years as fry in freshwater when they fed on sedges.

SILVER PETTICOAT

Tube: $1/2$" brass or copper tube
Tail: Fibres of the Mylar tubing teased out
Body: Silver Mylar tubing
Wing: Yellow bucktail tied short with a few fibres of orange and black bucktail over
Head: Black

From observations in recent years, it appears that salmon sometimes want the fly fished well below the surface. The Silver Petticoat was invented for Finlough at Delphi by Franz Schäfer of Munich. It has the advantage of being small and compact for casting and it fishes well, on the point, the copper tube and sparse dressing allowing it to sink quickly.

CURRY'S RED SHRIMP

Hook: Sizes 6–14 single, double or treble
Tag: Fine oval silver tinsel
Tail: Golden pheasant red breast feather
Rear body: Red floss
Rib: Fine oval silver tinsel
Veilings: Red hackle points or red swan slips
Middle hackle: Silver tipped badger
Front body: Black floss
Rib: Fine oval silver tinsel
Wings: Jungle cock – as eyes on the smaller sizes
Front hackle: White-tipped badger
Head: Red

Pat Curry's Red Shrimp has certainly proved its worth down the years. It is still as popular as when it was first tied over 50 years ago. Even though it was originally conceived as a river fly, it is highly effective on the lough when fished on the point, particularly for spring salmon.

7

Choosing the Right Tackle

for Ireland's Rivers and Loughs

Most people adopt a compulsive approach to flyfishing tackle. They think, 'I'd like to take up flyfishing and so I must buy a rod, reel, line and some flies'. That is wrong! The person who adopts this approach usually ends up with an outfit that is unsuited for the kind of fishing they want to do. They have chosen their tackle in the reverse order, beginning with the rod and that is not correct.

When selecting flyfishing tackle, it is important to understand that it must matched. The two basic requirements of flyfishing are matching the tackle and learning to cast.

The first thing to be considered is the kind of fishing that you are going to do most frequently. This will determine the kind and size of flies that you will use.

Next choose the line that will properly carry your flies to the fish.

Choose your Flyline

A flyline performs two functions. The first is that it is the weight that loads the rod. The flyline was once described by the American casting instructor, Lefty Kreh, as a long flexible weight that loads the rod and unrolls when it is cast out over the water. Its other function is to transport the fly.

Fishing flies come in a range of sizes from tiny smuts used for river trout to the great big heavy flies used for spring salmon fishing which are dressed on brass or copper tubes up to three inches long.

Using the analogy of the transporter, you would not use a low-loader to transport a piece of light furniture nor a pick-up truck for a bulldozer. So it is with flylines. A light line will carry a light fly, but not a heavy one. If a heavy line is used to cast small flies it will cause too great a disturbance on the water and frighten the fish.

Flylines are graded by weight according to a specific scale known as the AFTM (American Fishing Tackle Manufacturers' association) scale. Nowadays the scale ranges from AFTM 0 to AFTM 15. The precise point on

Left
Stuart McTeare selects flies for a day on Lough Sheelin. In assembling your tackle, the fly should be your starting point.

151

the scale into which a flyline fits is calculated by weighing the first thirty feet of the line, not counting the level tip. Thus a double taper No.4 floating line (DT4F) is much lighter than a double taper No.10 floating line (DT10F). For practical purposes, I tend to group lines into three categories – light, medium and heavy. My first grouping is AFTM 1 to 5. These are the light lines used mainly for river fishing and in practice, the most useful of these are AFTM 4 and AFTM 5. The medium weight lines are AFTM 6, 7 and 8. AFTM 6 and 7 are ideal for lough fishing from a boat and may also be useful for river sea trout, while AFTM 7 and 8 suit low water summer salmon fishing. AFTM 9 to 12 are the heavy lines. AFTM 12 is the heaviest you would ever require for fishing in Ireland and, together with AFTM 11, it is best suited to casting big tubes and Waddingtons.

I suggest that if you are going to use small trout flies on a river, where gentle and delicate presentation is required to avoid frightening the trout, then you will need a light line in the AFTM 4 to 5 size category. If, on the other hand, you want to cast a big heavy tube fly with ease, you will need a line capable of carrying it comfortably and AFTM 11 would be minimum. For medium sized flies, particularly the big doubles and trebles, a line from AFTM 8 to 10 is recommended. Once you have decided the size of fly or flies you will be fishing, then you can select an appropriate line weight.

Always remember that a light line is not capable of transporting a heavy fly to the target, nor is it practical to use a heavy line to cast a small fly. The heavy line will land on the water with such a splash that it defeats the whole purpose of the small fly which should land as lightly as thistle down on the water. First determine the kind and size of the flies you intend to fish and then choose the line that will transport them properly.

Flylines come in a number of profiles, the most common being double taper lines, weight-forward, Spey lines and shooting heads, sometimes also referred to as shooting tapers and level lines.

Lines have codes so that you can identify them. The following symbols usually appear on the packaging of a new line and tell you the kind of line it is:

DT - Double taper
WF - Weight-forward
ST - Shooting taper
SH - Shooting head
F - Floating
S - Sinking
WT - Wet tip or sink-tip
L - Level

Lines come in a range of densities, which include floating, intermediate, slow sink, fast sink, super fast sink and sink-tip or wet-tip. In all cases, the AFTM weight rating applies. This means that the first 30 feet of a DT6F weighs exactly the same as the first 30 feet of a DT6 fast sinking line.

LINE PROFILES

Double Taper Lines

Double taper lines, as the name denotes, have a taper at both ends. They give a stable casting loop and are the easiest lines to control. For this reason, they are highly recommended, particularly for the beginner. They are excellent for river trout fishing where good line control and gentle fly presentation is all-important.

The second use for double taper lines is on the double-handed salmon rod. In recent years, new 'Spey' type lines have been designed specially for these rods. However, particularly for the beginner, a double taper line facilitates good line control and better fly presentation.

An added bonus of the double taper is that it can be reversed when the working end becomes worn.

The advantage of a tapered line over a level line is that when a flyline is being cast properly with the rod, it forms into a U-shaped loop which turns over and straightens out, depositing the fly gently at the extremity of the leader. Level lines are difficult to turn over and even when they do so successfully, they do so with a sharp smack which is likely to disturb fish.

Weight-Forward Lines

These have only one taper – at the working end. This leads into a heavy portion of line, about 35 feet, concentrated at the front end. This is followed by thin, level 'running' line of similar material. Having the weight concentrated at the front of the line near the fly allows the angler, when making a cast, to release (shoot) line and the heavy portion will drag it along for a ride. In the hands of an experienced fly caster, it has the advantage of being able to carry a fly further. However, in a practical fishing situation, the difference in the distance achieved compared with a double taper line does not appear to be great. For the inexperienced flyfisher, a weight-forward line can be difficult to control resulting in unstable loops and sloppy casting.

Shooting Heads

Shooting heads, also referred to as 'shooting tapers', originated in the United States. They have gained a certain amount of acceptance among anglers who need to cast long distances from the banks of reservoirs or indeed on big salmon rivers. The shooting head is a sort of 'souped up' weight-forward line. It consists of thirty to forty feet of custom made weight-forward line as a front section attached either to low memory monofilament, braided monofilament or some other thin line that does not tangle easily. When the angler prepares to cast, the heavy line is drawn up to within about two feet of the tip ring of the rod, but not into it. When the forward cast is made and the line released by the angler, the tapered head drags the thin line along for a ride and great distances can be achieved,

using the double-haul casting technique. While shooting heads can be pur-chased custom-made, anglers can make up their own outfits by using half a double taper line (floating, slow sinking or fast sinking) or the front of a weight-forward line. This is not an outfit to be used by the beginner. In most situations 30–35 foot line 'heads' are easier to control and fish. To avoid getting caught up in bankside vegetation, a line tray should always be used.

ABOVE
Basic tackle for the lough: a spool of 6lb nylon, floating flyline, a 10-foot rod, reel and a plastic box of bushy flies. Stand by to catch trout, sea trout or even a salmon!

Level lines

These have the same thickness from end to end. As casting lines they are inferior to tapered lines and have almost disappeared except as thin shoot-ing lines for use with shooting heads.

CARE OF FLYLINES

The finished surface of modern flylines is smooth, enabling it to glide effortlessly through the eyes of the rod. However, with every day use, the line picks up grime that adheres to the surface. It can be dirt either from the bank and floor of the boat, or algae from the water. This reduces a line's efficiency when casting and so they need to be cleaned from time to time. This is best done by immersing the working portion of the line for 15 minutes in clean, tepid water with a little washing up liquid added. Then pull the line through a soft wet cloth and finally rinse in cold water. Allow it to dry by hanging it in loose coils over the back of a chair and then apply one of the flyline dressings available on the market. A clean freshly dressed line shoots effortlessly through the line guides and adds yards to the angler's cast. Because of the function it performs, a clean supple flyline is a wonderful aid to good fly presentation. Poor quality, neglected lines are an abomination, particularly for the beginner.

THE BUTT PIECE

BELOW
A well-stocked fly box like this is ideal for the boat, but the river angler will want something more compact and portable.

We have noted the advantage of the taper of the line in allowing the smooth transfer of energy right out to the end as the loop turns over. But it does not stop there. That energy must reach the fly through the leader. If the leader is tied directly to the end of the flyline, there is a severe breakdown in the transfer of energy from the flyline to the leader. A butt piece facilitates a controlled transfer of energy to the leader.

The original butt piece consisted of a two foot length of 20lbs to 25lbs monofilament needle-knotted to the end of the line, with a double over-hand loop at the end of which the leader is attached. It should be renewed at the start of every season. This is the butt piece I still prefer for all my wet fly and salmon fishing.

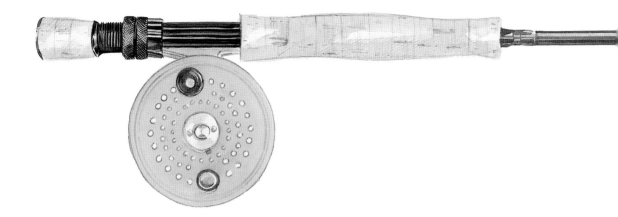

Short braided loops are a relatively recent invention. They come in 6-inch lengths and are attached to the flyline using a plastic sleeve. My impression is that they do little or nothing to assist in the turn over of the leader. On the contrary, they add weight to the end of the flyline – thereby having a negative effect on the taper – and in the case of light lines, such as AFTM 4, they have a positively detrimental effect by causing the end of a light flyline to dip sharply when the cast is made. I would only ever use them on heavy lines (AFTM 10–12) with a heavy monofilament or tapered braided sinking leader.

Tapered braided leaders are a different matter. They are attached in the same way as braided butts and they vary in length from 4 to 9 feet. A tippet of monofilament is added. They come in a range of densities, from floating to fast sinking. The floating version has little to recommend it. It is not suited for wet flyfishing where three or four flies are used. The sinking versions I find useful, particularly for salmon fishing and I often add a fast sinking braided leader to a sink-tip line when I want to achieve greater depth, particularly in early spring.

Most modern fly rods are made of carbon fibre and will carry a mark to show the weight of flyline to which they are best matched. The reel is little more than a line container and my preference is for ones with a single action and exposed rims (above).

THE FLY ROD

The fly rod is the most expensive part of the equipment. It behoves us, therefore, to choose wisely and be informed of our requirements. Most modern rods are made of carbon fibre. This in itself is no guarantee of excellence nor is the fact that it carries a particular brand name. Every angler should understand how a fly rod works and equip him or herself with one that best suits them and the kind of fishing they want to do. When selecting a rod – indeed when selecting an outfit – it is best to have someone to help you, like a qualified fly casting instructor whom you know is competent.

Having decided on the weight of line that best suits your requirements, the choice of fly rod is the next consideration. It must match the flyline. Just as flylines have an AFTM rating, fly rods also have their own rating system. In spin fishing, you cannot cast a heavy 6-inch metal lure on a

light spinning rod. The rod would not handle it. Similarly, a rod designed for throwing such a heavy lure won't load up enough with a light spoon or spinner to allow you to cast. The same principle applies to flyfishing. The rod is matched to a specific weight of line and it is only that particular line that it casts with greatest ease. Most modern rods will cast a line one weight lighter or heavier than the one that matches it perfectly. The weight of line that a rod can handle is usually marked beside the manufacturer's name above the cork handle thus: #7 or #7/8. Once you have determined what flies and line you need, then you should look for a rod with a matching number. Where a range of line weights are indicated, anglers are well advised to choose the heavier line. Rods are rated for 10 yards of line outside the rod tip (plus whatever small amount of level line has been allowed for between tip and start of taper). In all my years as a casting instructor, the most common problems experienced by my pupils are caused by mismatched tackle – in particular, flyline that is too light for the rod.

ROD ACTION

The most important feature of a fly rod is its 'action'. Rods come with a range of actions – progressive, butt, tip and everything in between. In everyday language, this means how stiff or soft a rod is when it bends and how it bends – hence the terms: 'tip', 'butt' or 'progressive' action. Volumes have been written about rod actions – parabolic, fast, slow, full flex, mid flex, tip flex, compound tapers, etc. It all means very little to the average angler. What he or she wants to know is how to find a suitable rod to go fishing!

Basically, a suitable rod is one that feels good when a line is cast. The reason it feels good is because it controls the line well. It becomes an extension of the angler's forearm and hand and places the fly with ease where the angler wishes. To find such a rod, we have to depend not only on the designer and manufacturer but also on an informed assessment of a rod. This is best done by putting a matching line on the rod, taking it to the water and trying it out. You wouldn't buy a car without first taking it for a drive. So it should be with a rod. If you don't feel competent, have someone advise you whom you know is competent. Most fishing tackle dealers will help. Buying a rod from a catalogue or mail order is a risky business, unless you have tried and tested a similar model. There are lovely rods on the market and there are dreadful rods too, ranging in price from a bargain to the indecently expensive. The most expensive rod does not necessarily mean the best rod. There is no substitute for having a rod tested by a qualified and competent person to determine its action and suitability.

There are some basic guidelines to follow. Butt action or full flex rods have a slow action. They are best suited to close range, delicate casting and

157

because they respond well to a gentle casting stroke, they are particularly suited to people learning to cast. The slow action is ideal and it reduces the number of casting faults. They are especially suited to protecting light tippets because of the full flex shock absorption. I like them a lot for small stream dry fly work.

Progressive or mid flex action allows for ease of casting and it will put the fly down gently. It is the best all-round action and hence is preferred for double-handed salmon rods and a wide range of single-handed trout rods. It is a good choice for the angler who needs one rod for a variety of conditions and can be relied upon to perform well.

Well designed tip action or tip flex rods give high line speed and perform best in the hands of competent fly casters. They give the tightest casting loops and are excellent for long range work and presenting a fly at a distance. They can be especially accurate, feel light and work best with short, quick casting strokes. As such, they are especially suited to double-hauling. The strong butt section gives them a lot of 'backbone' (in the upper weights) for playing big fish. I like this type of rod for salmon fishing with a single-handed rod. However, this action does not suit double-handed rods. They are both tiring and difficult to fish.

Rods, like everything else in this world, are governed by the laws of

ABOVE LEFT
Evening light on Lough Sheelin. At calm times like this, when small dry flies are called for, you appreciate a floating line that really floats.

physics. Designing and making a good rod is like making a good musical instrument. It is a great art.

ROD LENGTH

The correct length of a rod depends on the type of fishing and where an angler fishes. Overgrown trout rivers can only be fished with short rods, 7 to 8 feet long. Dry fly fishing on rivers is best done with 8 to 9 foot rods. Wet fly fishing on wider rivers calls for a 10 foot rod. Wet flyfishing from a boat calls for a long rod – 10 to 11 feet – depending on the strength of the angler's arm. Too long a rod and the leverage results in fatigue. 9–10 foot is ideal for dry fly fishing from a boat.

Salmon fishing, whether on lough or river, can be done with a range of rod lengths. For boat fishing, 9–11 foot rods will do. Double-handed rods are particularly tiring to fish from a boat. It is possible to fish some rivers in low water with a suitably rated 9 foot rod or any single-handed rod up to 11 foot. In high water and on the bigger rivers, double-handed rods make for easier casting and better line and fish control. In Ireland, depending on the size of the river, the length can vary from 13 feet to 16 feet.

With regard to the longer rods, one must never make the mistake of matching the rod to the river. The rod must always match the angler. This is the final match, in matching flyfishing tackle. Rods are made for anglers – not rivers. Fly casting can be strenuous and taxing at times and we all

BELOW RIGHT
A robust landing net is an essential item when boat fishing, for you never know when it might be required for a large trout or even a salmon.

must accept our limitations. People of slight build should choose a rod that they are able to handle with ease and comfort.

FLY REELS

A fly reel is primarily a container for holding line and secondly an aid when playing and landing big fish.

The first requirement of a reel is that it is big enough to hold the fly-line and sufficient backing. Sufficient backing can mean 50 yards for trout fishing to 150 yards on a salmon reel. The reel should be comfortably full when fully loaded.

Reels with an exposed rim are best. When playing a big fish, it is possible to apply even pressure on the rim with the palm of the hand – and more important, release it quickly when necessary.

My preference is for single action reels. That means that by turning the handle once, the drum rotates once. The alternatives are geared reels and automatic reels. Both of these can cause unnecessary problems, particularly for beginners. Keep the reel simple and there is less to go wrong.

Regarding winding the reel, my preference is to always use the non-fishing hand. An angler who fishes with the right hand should wind in line with the left hand. This avoids having to transfer the rod to non-fishing hand when playing a fish. The non-fishing hand is generally weaker, is unfamiliar with the feel of the rod and therefore has less control.

Most reels are supplied set up for right hand winding but have the facility to be easily changed from right to left hand winding by altering the mechanics.

The tension of the ratchet should be such that it is not too tight to cause a break of the leader, nor too free-running to cause the reel to over-run. While some reels can cost a lot of money, it is possible to find quite adequate models at a reasonable cost that contain all the desirable features listed above.

RIGHT
A perfect wild trout from the Corrib, with pronounced spots, small head and sharp edged fins. Tackle will never be more than a means to this superb end.

8

FLY CASTING

Every flyfisher aspires to cast a line with grace and style. We admire those who do so with elegance and ease. They are obviously well practised, relaxed, confident and in complete control of their fishing tackle, particularly the flyline. 'Control' is the operative word. That is what fly casting is all about – using the fly rod to control the line.

Fly casting is the technique of manipulating the rod and line to propel an artificial fly out over the water and to place the fly where the fish can see it. This is known as fly presentation. If the angler struggles, his presentation will suffer and the possibility of success diminishes.

Fly presentation, one of the traditional skills of the flyfisherman, is governed by three factors:

◎ the ability to cast a fly delicately and accurately
◎ the ability to cast a reasonable distance
◎ the movement of the fly in or on the water

Now any reasonably co-ordinated person can learn to cast a fly. All that is needed is to acquire the correct tackle, take instruction from a qualified tutor, study the various techniques and get in lots of practice. There is no substitute for practice. It is time invested in learning and it will ensure your steady improvement.

Professional instruction is a great time saver. It cuts out a lot of the trial and error, sets your priorities and it should be a source of encouragement.

Good presentation is based on mechanical principles and requires not just hand-eye co-ordination but harmonious interaction throughout the whole body. To make a good cast, the feet, legs, hips, waist, chest, shoulders, neck, upper and lower arms, wrist, hand and eyes must be as synchronised as they need be when hitting a good golf shot. Just as with the golf shot, the more synchronised the body movements, the better your fly presentation is likely to be.

PRACTICE MAKES PERFECT Students at one of my casting courses at Delphi refine their techniques with rod and line

THE TWO BASIC CASTS

There are many different casts, or should we call them methods of fly presentation, just as there are several different strokes in golf or tennis. They are used to facilitate fishing in different situations. All of them are governed by the same basic principles and are based on one or other of two casts, namely:

(1) The overhead cast
(2) The roll cast

When we cast a flyline, it travels out over the water in a loop.

The basic overhead cast involves two actions – the back cast, followed by a forward cast.

The roll cast relies on a single accelerating movement of the rod to propel the line forward in a loop.

Once the principles involved in making these two basic casts are clearly understood, then they can be applied to all other casts, e.g. the Double-haul, Spey cast, etc. Furthermore, they apply to the use of both single-handed and double-handed rods. It is a matter of getting the casting mechanics right.

LEARNING TO CAST

People take different routes in learning to cast. Some read books or magazine articles. Other watch instructional videos. By far the best way is to take casting lessons from a qualified instructor and understand and practice the basic principles. There is more to fly casting tuition than vague instructions like 'Start with the rod at eight o'clock, lift to ten o'clock, stop at twelve o'clock, etc. etc.'. I have long decided that clocks are good for telling the time but if you wish to learn to cast a fly, there has to be a better way of doing it. Personally, I found casting instruction immensely helpful and enlightening, even after years of fishing. Reading the works of acknowledged experts like Lefty Kreh and Ed Jaworowski was helpful too in studying and learning about casting. They reduce fly cast-

MASTERING THE FIRST PRINCIPLE Get rid of the slack before commencing the backcast

164

ing to four basic principles which go as follows:

(1) You can't make the cast till you make the end of the line move.

(2) The line will go in the direction the rod tip was moving when it stopped.

(3) Continuously accelerate, then stop the rod.

(4) The further you move the rod, the easier it is to cast.

Let's briefly examine each of these principles in turn.

FIRST PRINCIPLE

'You can't make the cast till you make the end of the line move'.

'Always lift a tight line' is another way of saying this. In reality, what it means that if there is a lot of slack in the line, the rod tip cannot load because you don't have the full weight of the line against which to load it. Consequently, a lot of energy is wasted picking up the slack line.

In practice, this principle requires that you start with the flyline extended straight out in front from the rod tip. There must be no slack before commencing the back cast (see picture opposite).

The same principle applies to the forward cast. The line should extend straight out behind. A poor or sloppy back cast creates slack line and results in a poor forward cast.

SECOND PRINCIPLE

'The line will go in the direction the tip was moving when it stopped'.

The fly rod is a flexible lever and a caster uses it to drive the flyline smoothly to a high speed. It is the tip of the rod that is driven at speed. Casters must learn and always be conscious of the fact that the rod is the casting tool. When the cast is made and the rod is stopped, energy is transferred from the rod tip to the flyline and it is the release of the stored energy out through the rod tip that moves the flyline.

Therefore, when we are aiming our cast in a particular direction, we must always 'think tip'. The line will go in the direction the rod tip was moving when it stopped. In practice, this means that if you wish to cast a line upwards, the rod tip must be moving upwards when it stops. Similarly, if you wish to cast horizontally or downwards, you learn to ensure that the rod tip is moving in the appropriate direction when it stopped. The manner in which the caster drives the line (whether the line is cast in a wide loop or a narrow loop) is determined by the skill of the caster and the action design of the rod. This principle ensures that your fly always goes where you wish it to go. Conversely, if the fly is ending up somewhere you don't wish it to go, you ought to look at the direction the rod tip was moving when it stopped.

A good analogy that helps to get the rod tip moving in the right direction and ensure tight stable casting loops, is to consider the forward cast as a smooth, accelerating painting stroke drawn along the ceiling. Narrow loops are obtained if the rod tip and the flyline are driven in a straight line

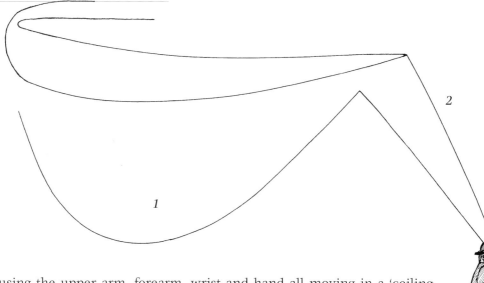

using the upper arm, forearm, wrist and hand all moving in a 'ceiling painting' motion. For short casts, use a short quick 'painting' stroke and for long casts and narrow loops, use a long straight-line rod tip painting stroke and a narrow loop will result.

THIRD PRINCIPLE

'Continuously accelerate, then stop the rod!'

The casting stroke is an accelerating stroke. Every cast should begin slowly, gradually accelerate, then come to quite a sudden stop.

The previous principles referred to the position of the rod tip and the tension in the line prior to commencing a cast. This one refers to the speed at which the rod moves during a cast and it is absolutely critical that the beginner understands it clearly and gets it right. It is essential to learn to stop the rod. Many beginners find it particularly difficult. The casting stroke is a special kind of stroke – a smooth progressive acceleration – most definitely not a swipe – followed by an abrupt stop and the lowering of the rod tip. On both the back cast and forward cast when the rod stops the line starts to bulge and race ahead of the rod tip to form the loop. We are here dealing with a mechanical action that must be performed correctly. In the language of an athletics coach, it is a motor action requiring practice to perfect the muscle memory.

The essence of this principle is that every good cast starts slowly and accelerates through a 'linear plane' to a stop. Trying to do it any other way, even using maximum force, will end in failure. Note the words 'linear plane'. If the rod deviates from this plane, particularly on the forward cast, both accuracy and distance will suffer due to the line travelling in an arc rather than straight forward.

FOURTH PRINCIPLE

'The further you move the rod, the easier it is to cast.'

THE BACKCAST
A poor backcast (1) creates slack line and will result in a poor forward cast. The rod should stop at (2) and allow the line to extend backwards.

166

To begin with, it is necessary to understand how a fly rod works. Basically, a fly rod acts as a lever and the load to be moved is the flyline. The further a lever moves, the more work it does. For a short movement and small angular rod rotation at the butt, the rod tip and line swings through a much longer distance at speed due to the lever length of the rod. The caster provides the energy for the rod tip to move the line. If the caster wishes to cast further (or into a strong wind) while using the same length of stroke, he must use either more force, or move the rod tip further. The use of short rod movements and more force puts the angler under increased pressure and leads to casting mistakes. Greater movement in the rod tip makes it a bit like a boy throwing a stone or an athlete throwing the javelin. If the athlete holds the javelin vertically above his head, he must explode with power to throw it any distance. By leaning backwards and reaching back with the arm and hand, he will achieve greater distance with less effort.

Similarly, with fly casting: short casts can be made by moving the rod tip a short distance. Long casts are achieved easier by moving the rod tip and line further and faster. The flyline gets speed from the very start of the cast and not at the end, from the unloading of the rod, as some think.

This means that, for seemingly effortless casting, you need to give the line plenty of lead. In other words, start the back cast with the rod tip held low and begin the forward cast with the rod held some distance behind the vertical.

All casts – overhead, into the wind, roll casts, Spey casts, etc. – employ these four principles. Once you master them, you will soon discover how easy and enjoyable fly casting and flyfishing can be.

THE BASIC OVERHEAD CAST

The basic overhead cast is performed with a single-handed rod. It will help enormously if the rod has a good action and is matched to the line.

These fly casting instructions are written with a right handed angler in mind.

GRIP

The rod handle is held – usually in the middle with the thumb placed firmly on top and the fingers underneath. Correct positioning of the thumb is very important. Don't squeeze the handle too tight.

STANCE

It is important to adopt a comfortable stance. This can vary from person to person. For short accurate casts, I'd suggest right foot forward. We'll develop this further when discussing dry fly fishing. For longer casts, stand with the right foot slightly back.

HOLDING THE LINE

Initially for beginners, I think it is better to hold the flyline trapped against the rod handle with the index finger of the casting hand. It is less distracting. When the caster becomes more proficient, the line can be held in the left hand. The purpose of holding the line is to keep it tight or anchored while casting. When holding the line in the left hand, the hands should not move too widely apart when casting. Rather, the left hand should follow the right, keeping the distance constant.

The basic overhead cast is the first cast a beginner should learn. Before beginning to practice, attach a 9 foot length of monofilament leader to the flyline and on the end, tie a short length (1 inch) of wool to simulate a fly.

The basic overhead cast (and all similar casts) consists of two parts: a back cast and a forward cast.

To make a basic overhead cast, extend 20–30 feet of flyline out in front of the rod tip and hold the tip low to the ground. Holding the line trapped against the rod handle (or in the left hand), slowly begin to raise the hand and forearm while at the same time elevating the point of the rod. As the thumb reaches eye level, accelerate the tip of the rod backward and stop it behind the vertical. Pause momentarily to allow the line to straighten on the back cast. The backcast is now complete. Now accelerate the rod tip forward to a stop and then continue to 'follow through' or drop the rod tip below the horizontal. This completes the forward cast.

To make the basic overhead cast and all other casts related to it, the angler first swings the rod using rotary and linear movements of the upper and lower arm, wrist and hand, directed towards driving the rod tip and flyline in the direction of the back cast. In an overhead cast, the rod is swung

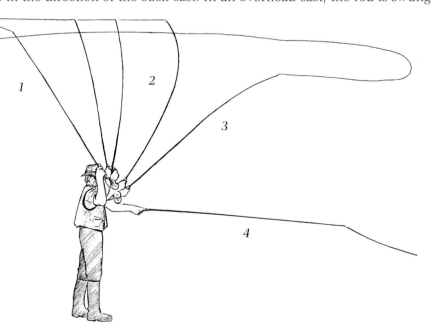

FORWARD CAST
From the back stop position (1) accelerate the rod tip forward (2) to a stop position (3) and then continue to follow through or drop the rod tip below the horizontal (4)

vertically. In doing so, for a small angular rotation of the rod butt, the rod tip and line will swing through a much longer distance at speed due to the lever length of the rod. The pull of the line on the rod tip bends the rod and the rod tip and line accelerates to a high speed. The rod is then stopped and bounces straight as the line rolls out on the back cast.

At the start of the forward cast, the rod is straight and not loaded. Contrary to popular belief, the back cast does not load the rod. It extends the line straight out from the tip in preparation for the forward cast. The tug felt at the finish of the back cast is due to the transfer of flyline momentum to the rod tip and then the rod bounces straight. For the forward cast, the angler swings the rod forward driving the rod tip and line in a straight line – the 'ceiling painting' action. The rod tip does not arc. As it is driven forward, the rod tip accelerates from zero at the start to a high speed just prior to where it stops. The spring in the rod unloads, driving the rod tip and line forward in the direction of the cast.

Beginners may find it difficult both to drive the line forward in a straight line and at the same time to achieve good acceleration. Instructors often advise aiming to cast the fly towards the horizon or the top of the far bank to overcome the first problem. To improve rod acceleration followed by a stop, the desired result may be achieved if the pull of the line on the rod tip is considered to be a 'piece of mud' that is flicked forward out of the rod tip as the cast is made.

Excessive movement of the wrist can cause severe problems for beginners. Hence, they are exhorted to keep a stiff wrist. This has the effect of limiting casting potential. It is much better to employ the use of an 'educated' wrist as this helps enormously in the final acceleration of the rod tip by tilting the butt forward just before the rod is stopped.

Circular wrist motion or circular arm action is the antithesis of the 'painting the ceiling' stroke. Both result in deep billowing loops that are difficult to control and quite useless.

COMMON FAULTS

1. Tailing loops, wind knots and the fly catching in line.
Likely causes: Tailing loops and related problems are caused by a variety of casting faults such as snapping the wrist and shocking the rod to achieve greater distance. They can also be caused by throwing the back cast too high or by pushing the hand forward as the rod is stopped. A smooth, accelerating forward cast followed by a dropping of the rod tip eliminates the problem.

2. Low back cast and line striking ground behind.
Likely causes: Failing to stop the rod on the back cast, too long a pause, or too little power in the back cast.

3. Line striking angler or rod tip on forward cast.
Likely causes: As 2 above, a low back cast, failing to stop the rod on the back

cast or too long a pause on the back cast.

4. The line fails to straighten, piles up, falls zig-zag fashion or fails to go out.

Likely causes: Lack of acceleration, failure to stop the rod in the forward casting stroke or cast aimed too low.

5. Line gives a cracking sound like a whip and point fly breaks off.

Likely cause: Too little power in back cast and commencing forward cast before the line has straightened behind.

6. Line slapping down on the water.

Likely cause: Lack of acceleration and lack of stop in the forward cast or the forward cast aimed too low.

SHOOTING LINE OR GAINING DISTANCE

Increasing the length of the cast is part of fishing. Once you have learned to control and cast 20–30 feet of line, it is possible to shoot extra line. This is done by stripping line off the reel and laying it on the ground. Make an overhead cast in the usual way and just as you stop the rod on the forward cast, release the line held in the left hand. You will find that several extra feet of line will shoot out of the tip eye. Shooting line effectively depends on how well you co-ordinate the stop of the right hand and releasing line.

The most common fault encountered here is releasing the line before the rod is stopped. With practice, the co-ordination will improve.

THE FALSE CAST

A false cast is a forward cast in which the line is not allowed to land on the water. It is used to increase line speed, to extend line, to change direction while casting, to dry the fly or line when dry fly fishing or to measure distance without setting the line on the water and thereby disturbing the fish.

To make a false cast, make a normal back cast and a forward cast, but before the forward cast extends fully, make another back cast and then make the final forward cast on to the water.

Excessive false casting is counter productive, except when drying a fly. One false cast should be adequate and two false casts should be the maximum that are required.

THE DRY FLY CAST

The dry fly cast is all about accurate and gentle presentation of the fly and, in most instances, preventing the fly from dragging. It is basically a short, accurate overhead cast.

THE SLACK-LINE CAST

The slack line cast is a casting technique to prevent the line dragging the dry fly across the current or downstream faster than the current. It is used

UPSTREAM DRY FLY CASTING is probably the most demanding of all. It requires great accuracy, straight delivery and a full extension before the flyline drops gently on to the water surface.

when casting the fly across fast running water to slower water or an eddy on the other side. Once you have stopped the rod on the forward cast, flick the rod tip smartly to the right or left. This will send a bend down the line as it falls on the water. If you want the bend near the end of the line, flick the rod sideways as you stop it on the forward cast. To make a bend closer to the rod tip, delay the flick a little. With practice the Slack Line Cast can solve a lot of drag problems.

THE CHECK CAST

The Check Cast is another technique used to prevent a dry fly dragging on the river. Two methods are used to achieve a Check Cast. The first is to cast the fly in the normal way. After you stop the rod on the forward cast, the hand and forearm are extended forward and as the line straightens, the elbow is pulled back sharply to the body. The line will drop on the water in a series of small curves but the fly will still reach its target accurately.

The second method is to make the forward cast in the normal way and just before the line finally turns over, pull or check the line with the line hand.

THE SIDE CAST

This is a good cast for studying your casting technique. It allows you to watch both the back cast and forward cast. It can only be performed when there are no obstructions at ground level and is used to cast a fly under an overhanging obstacle or to defeat a strong wind from behind.

Stand at right angles to the target, feet well apart. Hold the rod in the normal way – thumb on top and fingers underneath. Now turn the hand so that the palm is facing upwards. The reel will be facing forward with the thumb behind the handle. Now make a back cast in the horizontal plane watching the line straighten to the back and follow it with a forward cast in the same plane. By starting with the rod to the left, you can practice long strokes and see and feel the benefits of a long smooth accelerating lead. With a little practice, you will reach the target every time.

A common fault with this cast is to allow the rod tip to rise too much above the horizontal plane.

THE BACKHAND CAST

The Backhand Cast is used when an adverse wind blowing from the right, or bankside obstructions make the ordinary overhead cast dangerous or difficult. It can also be used in a drifting boat on a lough to avoid tangling with an angler on the right. This is a very useful cast and one with which every angler should be familiar.

To begin, correct stance and grip are important. Stand with the right foot well forward. Hold the rod with the thumb on top and slightly tilted to the left. The back cast is performed over the left shoulder with the back of the hand passing close by the left cheek. Meanwhile, the angler's weight is transferred on to the left foot. The rod is held with the thumb behind the rod handle and the knuckles – not the back of the hands – facing in the direction of the next cast. Now make a forward cast transferring the body weight forward to the right foot as you do so.

The distance the casting hand can move is rather limited. For longer casts, this is overcome by adopting the correct stance – above – and transferring the body weight backwards and forwards as the cast is made.

CASTING INTO THE WIND

Contrary to popular belief, casting a fly into the wind is not difficult. It is essential that every river angler learns to do so if he/she is to fish competently in all wind conditions. It is easier to learn if a matched AFTM 8 or 9 outfit is used. A steady head wind should present no problems but a foul swirling wind can make casting difficult even for the best casters.

When commencing to cast, remember that a head wind assists wonderfully well with straightening the line on the tight back cast. This is a great benefit. Begin with the rod tip low and the line extended fully in front. Make a long, smooth accelerating back cast in the opposite direction to that from which the wind is blowing. The angle of the cast will vary according to the wind direction. Always aim to cast directly down wind. Don't attempt to slice the wind. Aim the back cast high and stop the rod

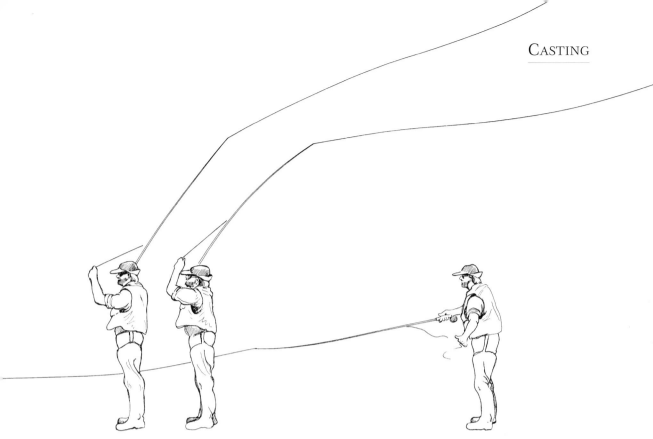

CASTING INTO THE WIND

Keep the back cast high and the forward cast pointing downwards

well back with the tip high. Now commence the forward cast and aim to turn it over inches above the water so that the wind can't get under it and blow it back. The forward cast should be of 'text book' quality – a long smooth accelerating stroke that delivers a tight, fast moving symmetrical loop (see page 168) with the rod tip moving in a straight line – 'painting a downward sloping ceiling' before it stops. Properly matched equipment and good technique facilitates casting against even very strong winds. When you learn to 'haul' cast a tight loop, the line will travel faster and also further.

THE TUCK CAST

The Tuck Cast is designed to aid a nymph or wet fly to sink quickly in the stream while being carried downstream on a slack leader.

The forward cast is made at a high angle (about 40^0 to the water) and the line is checked as it straightens (see Check cast, page 171). This causes the nymph to bounce back and fall vertically into the stream below.

THE DOUBLE-HAUL CAST

Most anglers have heard of and many aspire to learn the haul casts, both Single-haul and Double-haul. The latter is more effective and the one we will deal with here. When a haul is applied at the correct point in a cast, it increases line speed and hence distance. The haul is applied (by the hand holding the line) at precisely the moment the rod hand accelerates the rod

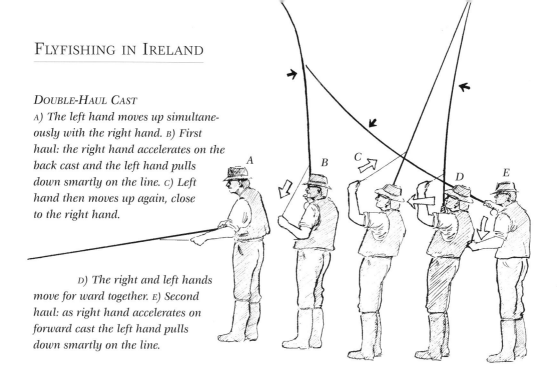

DOUBLE-HAUL CAST
A) *The left hand moves up simultaneously with the right hand.* B) *First haul: the right hand accelerates on the back cast and the left hand pulls down smartly on the line.* C) *Left hand then moves up again, close to the right hand.*

D) *The right and left hands move for ward together.* E) *Second haul: as right hand accelerates on forward cast the left hand pulls down smartly on the line.*

tip before the stop. The length of the haul varies to coincide with the timing demands of the rod being used. Short hauls are more effective when using fast tip action, quick-recovering rods. Long hauls are best suited to rods with progressive action.

To perform the Double-haul, stand with the left foot forward and the left shoulder pointing in the direction of the cast. With the line extended, hold the rod at waist level, pointing down the line. Commence the back cast in the usual way by raising the right hand and forearm. The left or line hand moves up with the right hand (see above). As the right hand accelerates the rod tip to a stop, the left hand simultaneously pulls down sharply on the line. It then moves up again – or rather, is pulled up close to the right hand – as the back cast unrolls. Because of the open stance the caster should be able to turn the head and watch the back cast. As the back cast is about to straighten, the forward cast commences and the right and left hands move forward together. Just as the right hand accelerates smoothly to a stop, the left hand pulls down smartly and simultaneously on the line and then releases the line at exactly the same time as the right hand stops the rod.

A good way to learn the Double-haul is to practice it in two parts on a lawn or sports field. First make the back cast with a haul and let the line fall to the ground behind. Now, think first about what you must do on the forward cast, rehearsing the actions in your mind and then make the cast. Finally, when you have grown accustomed to hauling in either direction, try to put the two casts together.

The Double-haul develops terrific line speed with very little effort when you learn to haul at exactly the same time as the rod hand reaches its final acceleration. Co-ordination and good casting form are the essential ingredients in making this cast well. It is best learned under the watchful

ROLL CAST

eye of a tutor and then followed with lots of practice. The Double-haul makes casting easier. Once learned, you will find yourself instinctively employing it in all sorts of situations, even for short and medium length casts.

THE ROLL CAST

The Roll Cast delivers a cast out over the water without making a back cast. Its main use is to straighten slack line or to lift a sunk line on to the surface prior to making an overhead or Spey cast. It can also be used to present a fly, especially when boat fishing on a windy day. Incidentally, the biggest Irish salmon I ever landed was taken after a roll cast. It is not possible to change direction appreciably with this cast.

To make a roll cast, begin with the rod tip low and the line extended out in front. Raise the forearm and hand and elevate the rod tip. The hand comes up level with and is drawn slowly back past the ear, pointing up and back (see above). The line is drawn slowly backwards with the fly feathering along the surface. It must not leave the water. Then pause momentarily. This allows the water to offer more resistance to the line and thereby loads the rod. Now proceed to make a normal forward cast. The line is cast in the direction you wish it to go and will unroll like a normal forward cast presenting the fly delicately.

For safety, always roll cast on the downwind side and if on a strongly flowing river, on the downstream side of the body to avoid accidents.

175

THE HAULED ROLL CAST

In order to get a lot of distance with a roll cast, it is necessary to learn to haul. The hauled roll cast can be used to shoot line upstream on a river by an angler standing in the water. It is particularly useful for the dry fly and also the upstream nymph in such situations where overhanging branches prevent the use of an overhead cast.

An upstream roll cast differs from one on still water or across a stream in that it must be performed with a quicker movement because of the flow of the river towards the angler. It is the resistance of the water on the line that loads the rod and for an efficient cast, the line must move faster than the water to create the increased resistance. In a fast flowing river, the line may leave the water momentarily, but must land again (as in a Spey cast) before the cast is completed.

The hauled roll cast is best practised initially on a still pool on a river or by a lough shore with the wind behind the learner. The whole idea is to increase the load on the rod tip and increase the line speed so that a tight loop is formed which unrolls fast and deposits the fly at the extremity of the leader and at a considerable distance. To achieve this, the angler makes a short quick pull on the line with the left hand at precisely the same time that right hand is accelerating the rod tip forward to a stop.

THE SWITCH CAST

A Switch Cast is made on a river, by an angler fishing down and across, where it is not possible, due to obstructions behind, to make a backcast. It is sometimes called a Spey cast but I think this term is best reserved for a similar cast with the double-handed rod. When practising, it is best learned by a right hand caster standing in the water near the left bank (looking downstream). Once learned, it can be made by the same angler from the right bank using a back hand switch cast that employs exactly the same mechanics. Since there is no backcast, it is based on roughly the same prin-ciples as a roll cast and the four basic principles of fly casting apply.

Begin by standing in the water a couple of yards from the left bank. Adopt an open stance with the left foot forward. Hold the rod pointing downstream with the line on the dangle. Then beginning very slowly, raise the rod tip to about 45°, releasing the belly of the line from the water and sweep the rod tip back in a horizontal plane making a weak side cast that causes the end of the line to fall on the water as close as possible to the angler and about opposite (but not below) where you are standing. The casting hand slows slightly as the line touches the water and then begins to accelerate a little further back and then forward into the forward cast. The loading of the rod comes from the loop of line that is thrown to the rear plus the traction of the end of the line on the water. It is important to extend the hand well to the rear to provide for a good long accelerating lead into the forward cast which can then be made with a fast tight loop aimed

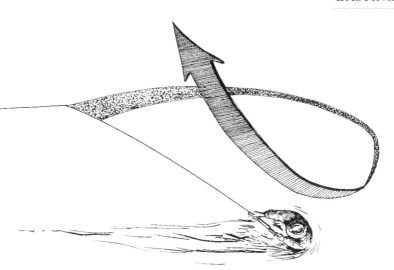

The Switch Cast allows the angler to change the direction of the cast without making a back cast (when there are obstructions behind, such as a tree or bank).

high across the river. Good timing is essential and this will come with practice. The result is well worth the effort. A very useful cast.

Warning: do not attempt this cast with a strong downstream wind.

THE DOUBLE SWITCH CAST

Actually this is not a real switch cast but rather a manipulation of the line to facilitate a roll cast across or down and across the river when the wind blows strongly downstream.

Begin to learn this cast standing on the right bank or in the river and adopt an open stance with the rod pointing downstream and the line on the dangle. Raise the rod tip eight or ten feet above the water to release the belly of the line from the water. The end of the line and fly must not leave the water. Now swing the point of the rod horizontally upstream extending the arm well to the left. The fly will now have been drawn up towards the angler but must not pass in front. With the same continuous stroke, flick the point of the rod outwards and bring the rod back downstream in front drawing the line with it. The outward flick of the rod tip is important as it positions the line correctly for the next stage of the cast. As the rod passes to the right of the caster, let it fall back into the roll cast position and proceed to make a forward cast.

This is a relatively easy cast to learn.

Precaution: don't attempt it with a strong upstream wind.

Mending the line In order to fish the fly at a correct speed it is essential to mend the line by flipping it upstream with the rod tip

THE MINI-ROLL

The mini-roll cast is a neat way of picking up a dry fly off the water with minimum disturbance and no disturbing drag of the leader. Holding the rod high and just in front of the vertical, flick the rod tip sharply in the direction of the line. This sends a small roll down the line. It will lift the fly from the water and you can then make the normal backcast.

CASTING WITH A DOUBLE-HANDED SALMON ROD

As the name indicates, both hands are used to grip the handle. This facilitates a greater input of energy by the caster. The rod is also longer than a single-handed rod. The popular lengths in this country vary between thirteen and fifteen feet. The longer rod means a longer lever action and the rod tip, of course, moves much further, thereby increasing the effectiveness of the fourth principle – 'the further you move the rod, the easier it is to cast'. At least that is the theory. In practice, observing the performance of some anglers using the long rod, it is easy to spot that a lot of the energy and effort is wasted. Yet, it shouldn't be. Casting with a double-handed rod should ensure long effortless casts.

WHERE TO BEGIN?

Unlike the single-handed rod, the range of casts is limited to the Overhead Cast, Roll Cast, Spey Cast, Double Spey Cast and the Snake Roll Cast. Of course, every river has two banks and the wind can blow strong from the left or the right. A competent caster with the big (double-handed) rod should learn to cast with the right hand up or the left hand up – in other words, over the right or left shoulder – not as daunting as one might think.

Before beginning to practice, attach a nine foot leader to the line and knot a piece of wool at the end to simulate a fly.

THE DOUBLE-HANDED GRIP

Let's assume that the caster is right handed. The butt of the rod fits comfortably into the palm of the left hand. The thumb is placed on top of the handle, pointing up the rod. The right hand is placed further up the handle – at shoulder width – with fingers underneath and thumb on top and pointing up the rod. The rod is now being held with the hands apart at shoulder width. This is important as it provides the perfect position for the rod to pivot during the final acceleration in a cast. The grip should be firm but not tight and the hands, forearms, upper arms and particularly the shoulders should be relaxed

By holding the line under the index finger of the right hand and taking it over the face of the reel to the left hand, the grip of each hand is equalised.

Double-handed grip

THE DOUBLE-HANDED OVERHEAD CAST

STANCE

Stand with the right foot well forward. At the beginning of the cast, most of the weight is on the front foot. During the cast, it is transferred to the back foot on the back cast and on to the front foot again for the final delivery of the forward cast.

The four casting principles laid down for the single-handed rod apply equally to the big rod. Only the mechanics of the cast differs due to the use of two hands.

To begin a cast, stretch out fifty or sixty feet of line in front and hold the rod tip low. Now, by raising the forearms, lift the rod and elevate the rod. The line is now coming off the water. The weight is now gradually transferred to the back foot as the rod begins to move back and the tip accelerates to a stop.

The acceleration is achieved by a controlled pivoting of the rod handle – the bottom hand tilts the rod butt forward and simultaneously the top hand tilts the handle backwards. When the rod stops, it should not recoil or upswing, a common fault with beginners. It is caused by too tight a grip and excessive tension in the caster's arms and shoulders. The problem is usually solved as the learner begins to relax. The caster's weight is now firmly on the back foot and he/she pauses while the loop unrolls.

For long casts, the rod tip may drift back. This increases the amount of lead available for the forward cast. Just before the line finally straightens, the body begins to lean forward, drawing the arms and rod with it. The arms then come more into play, moving forward, slowly and then quickening. As they pass the face, the final acceleration occurs – the hands pivot the handle – just as on the back cast. The burst of energy speeds the tip forward and the rod is stopped before being lowered to the fishing position.

The forward cast is a carefully co-ordinated movement involving the legs, body, arms and hands. It requires study, thought and a lot of practice. The reward is a long, symmetrical, tight, fast-moving loop that turns the leader over, giving perfect fly presentation.

Of course, in a fishing situation, at the start of a back cast, the line is rarely straight out in front of the rod. The river will have carried it downstream to the angler's right or left. Before commencing the backcast, the rod should be pointed in the direction of the next cast and proceed from that position into the back cast.

COMMON CASTING FAULTS WITH A DOUBLE-HANDED ROD

If an angler is having difficulties with the overhead cast, it follows that one or more things are not being done properly. The casting principles are being violated and energy is being wasted.
The most common faults are:
◎ Beginning the back cast with the rod tip held too high.
◎ The rod butt is allowed to protrude too far to the front on the back cast and the rod tip is not stopped.
◎ Stopping the rod tip too soon on the back cast.
◎ Causing the rod tip to recoil or upswing on the back cast.
◎ Too short a pause between the back cast and the forward cast.
◎ The rod describing too great an arc on the forward cast.

The Roll Cast

The roll cast is mostly used to straighten slack line to lift a sunk line on to the surface.

Stand with the right foot forward and rod tip close to the water. Raise the hands to face level and elevate the rod tip. Transfer the weight to the back foot and bring the hands back about level with the ear and take the rod tip back about forty five degrees behind the vertical. These actions will have drawn the line and fly along the surface of the water. The line falls in a big loose curve on the outside of the rod – away from the angler. If a floating line is being used, pause momentarily to increase the traction of the line on the water. If a sunk line is used, there is no need to pause. From here on the procedure is as for the overhead forward cast: namely lean forward, accelerate the rod tip forward, stop the rod and then follow through. Properly executed, the line will unroll and straighten as in an overhead cast. It is even possible to short line with a roll cast.

The Single Spey Cast

The Spey cast is essential for the angler who wishes to fish a stretch of river irrespective of tree lined banks or other obstructions behind that might impede a back cast. It offers the salmon angler the advantage that no line is projected behind. Of even greater importance is the fact that a properly executed Spey cast is extremely energy efficient and can be fished for hours without fatigue – even when overhead casting is quite possible. It is probably the most difficult of the casts to learn with the double-handed rod, requiring a thorough knowledge of the correct techniques for manipulating both rod and line, concentration and split second timing. When properly executed, it is possible to cast a fly every bit as far and as accurately as with an overhead cast.

Begin with the right hand up the rod and an open stance – standing in the water by the left bank of a fairly fast moving stream – the right foot pointing in the direction of the next cast. Turn the upper body and face downstream with the rod and line on the dangle and the body weight on the left foot. Raise the rod tip ten or twelve feet to release as much line as possible from the water. With a weak, oblique side cast, throw a loop of line behind you, without dipping the rod tip and simultaneously transfer your body weight to the right foot as you swivel the hips to face the forward cast. The arms extend well back and the end of the line falls in a straight line – not in a squiggle – on the water close to the angler and just upstream of the direction of the forward cast. The end of the line touches down at the same time as the arms extend fully and the rod points obliquely backward. The end of the line landing on the water, plus the energy imparted to the backward moving loop constitutes the load for the rod. In a well co-ordinated movement, the body moves forward and the arms draw the rod in a linear plane. As the hands finally pivot, the rod tip accelerates to an abrupt stop

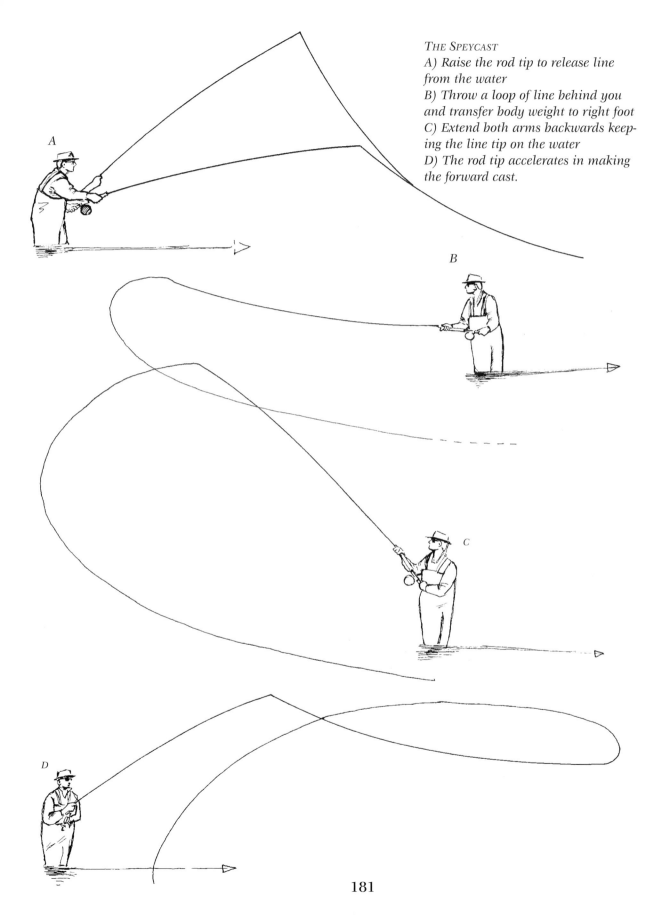

A

B

THE SPEYCAST
A) *Raise the rod tip to release line from the water*
B) *Throw a loop of line behind you and transfer body weight to right foot*
C) *Extend both arms backwards keeping the line tip on the water*
D) *The rod tip accelerates in making the forward cast.*

C

D

and a perfect loop of line shoots across the river.

This cast requires concentration, good timing and lots of practice. It is so energy saving that it soon becomes the regular cast used by the double-handed fisher, except when a strong downstream wind is blowing, in which case a Double Spey Cast is used.

THE DOUBLE SPEY CAST

This cast is used with a downstream wind blowing. It ought not to be used with an upstream wind.

To begin, the same hand should be up the rod as the bank being fished, i.e. right bank, right hand up the rod. The angler adopts an open stance, facing in the direction of the cast. The line will be on the dangle straight down from the rod point. Swivel the upper body, raise the rod tip and release as much line as possible from the water, but not the fly. Leisurely draw the rod tip obliquely across the front of the body and upstream, well away from the body and continue until it is slightly behind the angler and to his left, before bending the line outward and coming forward across the angler's front again. The rod tip continues the arc on the downstream side of the angler and proceeds back to a point well behind the vertical to begin the forward cast. During all of this manoeuvre, the fly at all times remains downstream of the angler. If the cast has been properly timed so far, the point where the airborne part of the line ends and the waterborne part begins is very slightly downstream of the angler. The forward cast is now made high across the river using the same technique as for the final delivery in a roll cast.

The end of the line, the leader and the fly remain in the water throughout the cast, it does not pass upstream of the angler and only leaves the water on the final delivery. It is therefore considered to be a very safe cast.

The Double Spey Cast utilises the four casting principles. It begins slowly, continues to build up momentum and accelerates to a stop before the rod is lowered. It is used when a downstream wind is blowing and for safety reasons should not be attempted with a stiff upstream wind.

DOUBLE-HANDED SPEY CAST
A bird's eye view of the casting movement. The arrowed line marks the path of the rod tip

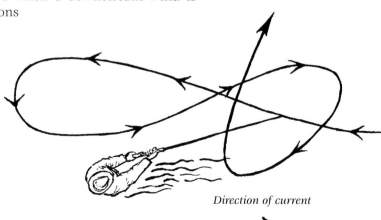

Direction of current

A Word about Knots

Tying knots is the bane of many anglers' lives, but like it or not, it must be done. Much of our tackle is held together that way. Some are tied infrequently like joining flyline and backing. Then there are the others that must be tied every time we go fishing – like tying on a fly. Now the angler who can tie all of his/her own knots is really self sufficient and can get on with the job at hand – namely fishing. The alternative – and it's a poor one – is to have someone do it for you. That is neither practical nor convenient. Remember the old adage 'Never water another man's whiskey, or kiss his wife' to which I would add 'or tie his knots' if you don't want to be blamed when someone else loses a fish.

Those knots that are tied infrequently are: attaching the backing line to the reel, tying the flyline to the backing and attaching the butt piece. You can have these tied in the tackle shop. But when it comes to the leader or cast (and I prefer to call it leader) the angler should become self reliant and competent.

It is as well to know a little about leader materials and their individual characteristics. Nowadays, there's not only nylon, but double-strength nylon, copolymer monofilament and fluoro-carbon monofilament (the latest high-tech low-diameter tippet material).

Everyone will have their own opinion about these new materials and no doubt their high-tech characteristics make it easier to catch trout and salmon. Personally, I prefer clear or green tinged monofilament in clear undisturbed water. Coloured monofilament may be used in peat stained or coloured water or in clean water where there is a big wave or a lot of turbulence. But one thing that monofilament of whatever kind will not tolerate is a badly tied knot. There are some knots that have better knot strength than others, but all knots must be tied correctly and this takes practice. Don't use too much pressure or cause friction. This will kink the leader. A well tied knot snugs together easily with all the turns even. Once a knot has been formed correctly on monofilament, it should be moistened – except PTFE-coated material – and then gently tightened. It is important that knots are not overtightened or tested to the point of destruction. Let the fish do that. If a knot does not look snug and well tied, cut it off and begin again. A badly tied knot will at best, reduce your leader strength by at least fifty percent and at worst it will slip, come loose and possibly loose the fish of a lifetime.

Wind knots on a leader should be undone as soon as they are noticed, using the points of two needles, and if they are too tight or the leader has signs of abrasion, it should be changed. Finally, all leaders should be rubbed down with a Fullers Earth compound to remove shine and prevent glint and help it to sink. The following is a selection of knots that I have used in different situations and found reliable over the years.

TURLE KNOT

This is the knot I recommend for tying on salmon flies. It has the advantage that the knot makes the fly swim in a straight line and doesn't allow it to twist at an angle

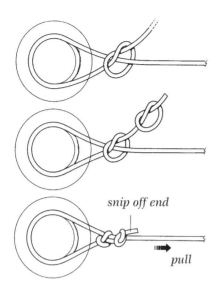

snip off end

pull

SPINDLE KNOT

For attaching backing to reel. Be sure to take the backing twice round the spindle. This will lock it firmly on the spindle when the knot is pulled tight.

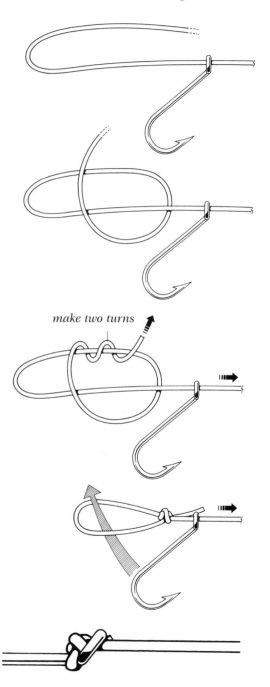

make two turns

FOUR-TURN WATER KNOT

(LEFT)

Sometimes known as the Surgeon's knot, this is a reliable one for joining two lengths of nylon, or for making a dropper. Works well on all strengths of nylon and monofilament.

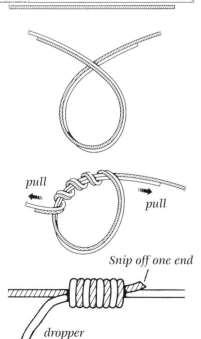

pull

pull

Snip off one end

dropper

NEEDLE KNOT

A good knot for attaching flyline (with braided core only) to butt piece, ensuring a smooth passage of line through the tip ring of the rod.

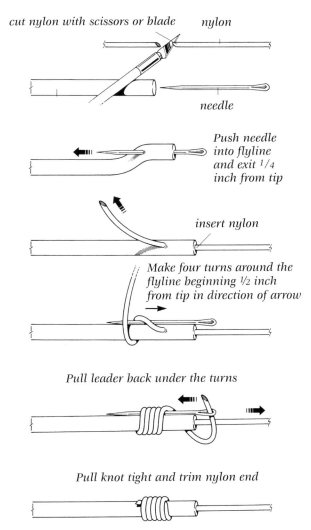

cut nylon with scissors or blade   *nylon*

needle

Push needle into flyline and exit ¹/₄ inch from tip

insert nylon

Make four turns around the flyline beginning ¹/₂ inch from tip in direction of arrow

Pull leader back under the turns

Pull knot tight and trim nylon end

NAIL KNOT

Constructed in the same way as the Needle knot, but this time the nylon is not inserted into the fly-line. Instead, it is wrapped tightly round it. Although known as the 'Nail' knot, I find a needle makes the tying easier.

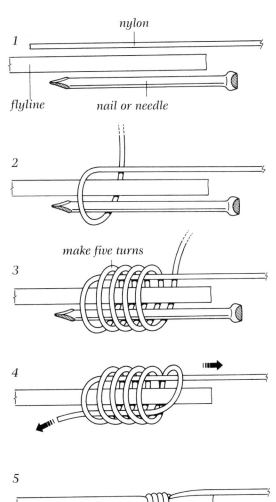

nylon

1

flyline   *nail or needle*

2

make five turns

3

4

5

NEEDLE & NAIL KNOT – COMBINED!

When your are fishing for big fish, such as salmon and large lough trout, which may test your backing knot, I recommend you to combine both these knots, spaced one inch apart when joining backing to line. This will give total reliability.

185

TUCKED HALF BLOOD KNOT

A sound and straightforward knot for attaching trout flies and small salmon flies to the leader

DOUBLE GRINNER KNOT

An excellent knot for joining two lengths of nylon.

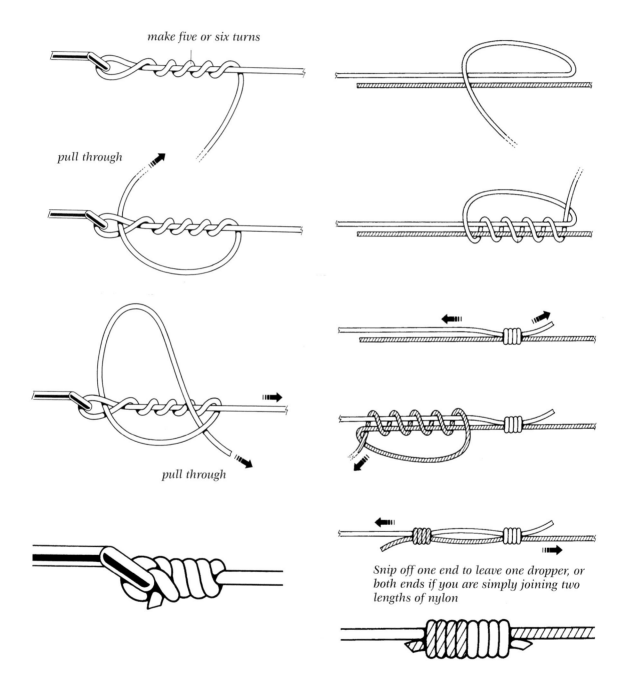

make five or six turns

pull through

pull through

Snip off one end to leave one dropper, or both ends if you are simply joining two lengths of nylon

EUGENE BEND KNOT

This is an excellent knot for attaching small dry flies to the leader.

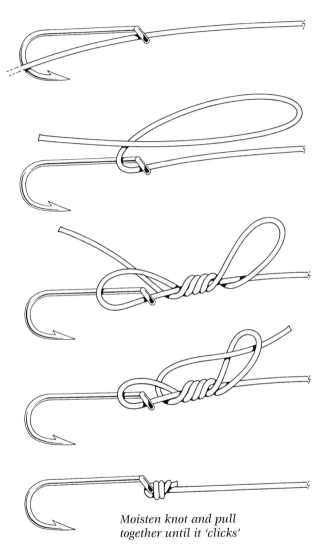

Moisten knot and pull together until it 'clicks'

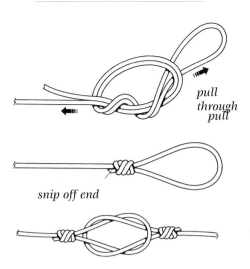

pull through pull

snip off end

DOUBLE OVERHAND LOOP *(ABOVE)*

Sometimes known as the Surgeon's Loop, this knot creates a permanent loop for the end of the nylon butt piece. It can also be tied at the top end end of the leader, making it easy to attach (and detach) the two by means of interlocking loops (see bottom picture above).

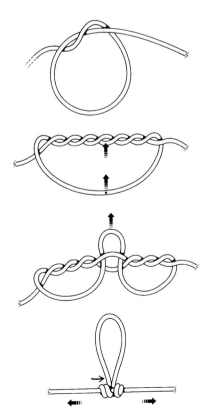

DROPPER LOOP KNOT *(RIGHT)*

A fast and reliable way to make a dropper – even in the dark. This is a knot I use a lot when using normal stretchy nylon.

INDEX